£4

An Introduction to Co-dependency for Counsellors

Gateways to Counselling

Consultant editor:
Windy Dryden, Professor of Counselling at Goldsmiths
College, University of London

Series editor:
Maria Stasiak

Project manager:
Carron Staplehurst

The *Gateways to Counselling* series comprises books on various
aspects of counselling theory and practice. Written with the
assistance of the Central School of Counselling and Therapy,
one of the largest counselling training organisations in the
UK, the books address the needs of both students and tutors
and are relevant for a range of training courses, regardless of
specific orientation.

Other books in the series include:

STARVING TO LIVE
The paradox of anorexia nervosa
Alessandra Lemma-Wright

COUNSELLING SKILLS FOR PROFESSIONAL HELPERS
John Pratt

COUNSELLING IN A GENERAL PRACTICE SETTING
James Breese

ON LISTENING AND LEARNING
Student counselling in further and higher education
Colin Lago and Geraldine Shipton

TRANSCULTURAL COUNSELLING
Zack Eleftheriadou

AN INTRODUCTION TO CO-DEPENDENCY FOR COUNSELLORS

Gill Reeve

Central Book Publishing Ltd
London

First published 1994
by Central Book Publishing Ltd
Centre House, 56B Hale Lane
London, NW7 3PR

© 1994 Gill Reeve

Phototypeset in 10 on 12 point Century Roman and Optima by
Intype, London.
Printed in Great Britain by
Tudor Printing, Park Road, Barnet.

Cover illustration by Helen S. Roper.

British Library Cataloguing in Publication Data

Reeve, Gill
Introduction to Co-dependency for
Counsellors. – (Gateways to Counselling
Series)
I. Title   II. Series
361.323
ISBN 1–898458–05–7

Contents

Introduction

Much has been written about childhood abuse, loss of self and addictions. Co-dependency is a relatively new theory and the first to link all three. The bulk of co-dependency literature comes from America and many of the books are written for the lay person rather than the professional. This may explain why counselling courses are only now responding to requests to include co-dependency on their itinerary.

This book is intended to go some way towards filling the gap which still exists, so that you can recognise and respond to the client who needs help with co-dependency.

One of the roots of co-dependency was in the foundation of Alcoholics Anonymous in America in the 1930s. The two founder members held frequent group support meetings and developed the '12-step' programme. These were twelve principles by which it was felt an alcoholic could recover, and included the spiritual concept of a power greater than the individual. Through emphasising alcoholism as an illness the social stigma was removed, as was the idea that willpower alone could enable an alcoholic to stop drinking. The focus on group support stressed the need for an alcoholic to reach out for help rather than struggling on their own, and to continue to help others by attending groups and offering their own experience as an example once sobriety had been achieved.

Other '12-step' programmes have evolved, based on the same principle as AA; e.g. Narcotics Anonymous, Gamblers Anonymous, Debtors Anonymous, Overeaters Anonymous. As a movement, it has influenced treatment methods for addiction, particularly in the USA.

One of the co-founders of AA, Bill Wilson, realised that

although he had achieved and maintained sobriety from alcohol, all was still not well, as he lacked 'emotional sobriety'. He recognised that he suffered bouts of depression because of his absolute dependency on other people or circumstances to make him feel good and that this dependency meant he tried to control both the people and conditions around him. As he began to let go of this dependency he was relieved of his depression more effectively than when he had tried antidepressants and drugs after he gave up alcohol. From today's understanding of co-dependency it seems as if Bill Wilson was formulating his own definition out of self-observed emotional problems, long before the word was first coined.

There have been criticisms of co-dependency. One is that it is merely a pop-psychology fad, too general in its application. A recent newspaper article described it as 'any sort of needy or dependent behaviour, whether connected to an addiction or not' (Zoë Heller, 'The road to recovery', *Independent on Sunday*, 14 June 1992). Whilst in its popular form it may have developed a jargon which can oversimplify complexities, there is a clearly defined theory and practice for co-dependency which has implications for many areas of counselling.

So, let me offer you my definition of co-dependency. Co-dependency is a loss of self as a result of adaptation in childhood to primary caregivers' needs over and above the child's. The adult is left with insufficient self-esteem and often doesn't know or cannot express their own thoughts and feelings. They have problems being interdependent and setting boundaries and often view life in extremes. They may be overcontrolling and have difficulty forming intimate relationships. To relieve the pain of the above symptoms co-dependents turn to something outside of themselves to create a greater internal comfort, be it drugs, gambling or another person. They become dependent on someone or something else to make them feel better and give them an identity. A sense of deep shame about who they really are is the main emotion which fuels co-dependency. They have probably developed a most convincing mask which means they are viewed by the world as strong and secure, when underneath lies self-doubt and depression. Obsession with this external source of internal comfort can become a priority and harmful consequences develop as other priorities are ignored. Removing the obsession or addiction is half the solution. The other half involves addressing both the adult symptoms of co-dependency and the old pain of childhood which triggers the need for the substance or behaviour. Recovery comes through the co-dependent discovering and accepting their real self.

Another criticism of co-dependency has been that the term could apply to everyone and that it is therefore meaningless.

Obviously most people do not come from a family which functions in a perfectly healthy way all of the time. At times of stress, or with certain people, any adult may exhibit behaviours which I have just described as symptomatic of co-dependency, e.g. pretend they are feeling confident when they are feeling afraid, feel unsure of their opinion or act in an overcontrolling manner. However, a person who is co-dependent will experience all these symptoms on a more or less daily basis and it is estimated by co-dependency counsellors that this condition affects approximately 10 per cent of the population.

Co-dependency theory was developed in American drug and alcohol treatment centres which were based on the 12-step programmes. As a result, co-dependency has become synonymous with this particular form of treatment, and those who find its methods unpalatable are equally quick to dismiss co-dependency. However, co-dependency, like alcoholism and other addictions, can be treated within or without 12-step programmes, if the counselling profession recognises and learns how to work with those it affects.

I want to summarise below how co-dependency theory and practice is relevant to many areas of counselling, all of which will be covered in more detail as you read on.

If you are working with addicts, co-dependency can be usefully viewed as an underlying symptom. Chapter 2 shows how the addiction is invariably used to cover up the pain of the client's co-dependency. The term 'addiction' is understood in its widest sense as explained below, and can include eating disorders, relationship addiction or alcoholism, to name a few examples. An understanding of co-dependency is useful if you are counselling a family or couple where an addiction exists. If you refer to Chapter 3 it will help you look at the addiction systemically and see the part played by other family members or a partner. It can help you to see their response as needing help in itself, rather than as an unhelpful obstruction to the addict's recovery.

Co-dependency theory offers a new way of looking at childhood abuse. In Chapter 4 I will show you how to deal with denial and prompt you to dig a little deeper when your client insists they had a normal, happy childhood. The theory offers a link between addictions and abuse and also points to new methods of healing the hurt, as in understanding your clients' 'inner child' and how your clients can reparent themselves.

Co-dependency theory examines relationships – both between people and with ourselves – and shows how loss of self can cause low self-esteem and difficulty with intimacy. Chapter 5 explores the basic premise that if we are out of touch with our true self because it has been shamed out of existence, we cannot have a good relationship with ourselves, because we feel ashamed of who we are, nor can we be safely intimate, because we are hiding who we are. The use of boundaries is one way of learning to feel safer with others and this chapter teaches this and other methods to help clients function better as adults.

Many counsellors are co-dependent, but we can nevertheless learn to be excellent counsellors if we keep working on our own co-dependency and keep a check on how and when it could intrude on our professionalism. Chapter 6 holds up the mirror for you to check your own co-dependency.

I think this shows that whilst co-dependency is a new theory, it is an exciting one and one that has much to offer various fields of counselling. I hope too I've whetted your appetite enough for you to move on to Chapter 1, where I'll be looking at how co-dependency developed as a theory and at its links with other theories.

1

The Development of Co-dependency and Links to Other Theories

The professional definition of co-dependency developed as a theory drawn from practice in American drug and alcohol treatment centres. The family or partner of a chemically dependent person was observed to have developed a way of coping with the addict and with their own life which was considered unhealthy and unhelpful. They experienced strong feelings of shame, pain or anger in relation to the addict but felt compulsively moved to become that person's caretaker. They denied the addict's addiction and also their own feelings. Whilst they believed the addiction was often their fault because they were helping imperfectly, once the addict achieved abstinence they became resentful and often sabotaged recovery. It became clear that whilst the addict was hooked on a substance or behaviour, the family or partner was hooked on the addict staying addicted. Remove the addiction from the addict and he or she suffered from painful emotions. And so did the family or partner. The latter were called co-dependents, the word meaning a person connected to another person dependent on a substance. Realising that this group of people needed help in their own right other 12-step programmes evolved in response. These include Al-Anon and Families Anonymous (for those involved with drug addicts).

However, research and clinical work on families which looks at family systems has shown that this coping mechanism, which is largely one of avoidance, can develop even if the person affected is not involved with an addict. It can develop in any dysfunctional family where unwritten rules dictate that a person grows up unable to develop his or her real self. For example, this could be a family where addictions exist, a family

1

where no one can express emotions, a family where it's not acceptable to make mistakes or ask for help or a family where physical or sexual abuse is occurring.

How does the theory of co-dependency link to other theories used in counselling and psychotherapy?

MENTAL HEALTH AND PERSONALITY DISORDERS

There is no entry under co-dependency in the DSM III (the *Diagnostic and Statistical Manual of Mental Disorders*). This book was last updated in 1980, which would explain the omission, but should it be there in future? Co-dependency has been described as a serious personality disorder (Mellody 1989: 215) and is considered to have links with established personality disorders such as 'dependent personality'.

Personality disorders are disorders of character rather than mood or thought, i.e., the sufferer will display the behaviour or trait all the time and not episodically. They can cause substantial impairment in how the person functions in social or occupational settings and erratic interpersonal relationships, as well as a great deal of personal distress.

Psychiatrists often view personality disorders pessimistically, seeing little hope of a cure in the form of medication or behavioural treatment. Humanistic therapists and counsellors are more inclined to see personality disorders as an adaptation to what has happened in that individual's life and are therefore more optimistic that change is possible.

In light of these definitions I suggest that co-dependency could be classified as a personality disorder, with the outlook that it is treatable and reversible, at least to a manageable degree, with therapeutic help.

However, whether it is helpful to classify it as such depends on how the term is used. Personality disorders are often used as psychiatric labels which persist for life, making the client likely to be dismissed as beyond help or hope. If its definition as a separate personality disorder meant that co-dependency was taken seriously as a condition in its own right there could be value in its future inclusion.

The development of co-dependency theory

DEVELOPMENTAL THEORY

An understanding of developmental theory is useful in showing us the stages of development which occur naturally in a healthy family and which a child must pass through and resolve if she is to become a healthy adult. Eric Erikson describes each stage as a 'crisis'. By this he means a critical period rather than an emergency, when the opportunity for increased awareness and development is at its peak. Once the child has resolved one stage she is then faced with the 'crisis' of the next, armed with the ego strength she has just learned.

Stage	Crisis	Ego strength
infant	trust v. mistrust	hope
toddler	autonomy v. shame and doubt	willpower
pre-school	initiative v. guilt	purpose
school age	industry v. inferiority	competence

Clearly if a child is unable to resolve these stages she will grow up unable to trust, riddled with shame, feeling guilty when she strikes out for herself and with a sense of inferiority – all common traits in co-dependent adults.

SYSTEMS THEORY AND FAMILY THERAPY

Systems theory is a body of thought derived from science which defines systems by the way they interrelate. Family therapy is relatively new and was developed in response to a perceived breakdown of the family and an understanding that an individual's problems rarely exist without having some source in disturbed relationships within the individual's family.

In the 1970s Gregory Bateson introduced a systemic approach to family therapy and this is now widely used. Treatment involves a shift from examining an individual's intra-psychic inner world to looking at the interactions within the family, which are often governed by the rules of that family's system. It means seeing the individual's problem as a family problem which has simply selected that individual for its expression.

This is particularly useful for addiction treatment. The family of the addict rarely see their role in perpetuating the

3

addict's difficulties, and prefer to see themselves as victims, whose lives would be so much better if only the addict would stop their addiction. If the addict is given therapeutic help to make changes the family may be oblivious to these changes and therefore unsupportive, or they may sabotage the client's efforts to change in order to restore the family *status quo*. Systemic family therapy stresses that change in any one part of a system leads to a related change in others, and would stress the need for the family to receive help too.

Once the family has achieved abstinence and stabilised their life without the addiction being a part of it, other problems of communication and relationships in the family, which were previously masked by the addiction, surface. These too are seen as needing a family approach, rather than being simply the ex-addict's individual neuroses.

Co-dependency can also be seen as a family problem, whereby healthy growth is obstructed by a set of rules within the family system. Systemic therapy is not just about seeing lots of people all at once! It is a theoretical framework and as such can be applied even if the counsellor is working with individuals. How to do this is beyond the scope of my book, but the counsellor can learn how to unearth a family's alliances and disputes so that whilst the family's role in maintaining a client's co-dependency is not blamed it is also not lost.

TRANSACTIONAL ANALYSIS

Eric Berne was the key figure in the development of transactional analysis, which emphasises the conflict between self-esteem and inferiority and the relation between the ego and the consciousness, using the ego states Parent, Adult, Child. People's 'scripts' and 'games' are examined, i.e., the way people use unhelpful messages and familiar transactions to remain feeling worthless.

These concepts can be helpful in working with co-dependency, particularly when looking at low self-esteem and at the false self. Berne's theory of the script is that it is derived from early experiences of the individual in her family, given that a child's main aim is to please her parents by finding out what it is they want of her and then trying to adapt to it. This is how the adapted child, or the false self, develops. Berne believed that to live free of the script a person has to throw away most of it and start again – the natural child is either free from, or in the process of freeing herself from, parental influences.

Berne thought that the more injunctions are given to a child, the more the child becomes tied to their script. In healthier families the child is given plenty of permissions, i.e., allowed to be free of their script. A co-dependency counsellor might follow Berne's line in seeing their role as giving their client the permissions she has not received from her parents. Ultimately the goal in co-dependency work is for the client to give herself these permissions through reparenting herself.

Co-dependency theory recognises how unhelpful it can be for the adult to be functioning from their inner child perspective, and in my book I look at ways a counsellor can help to draw out the healthy adult. Berne uses the words 'contamination' and 'exclusion' to identify when the Child ego or Parent ego are unhelpfully intruding on the adult or when any of the ego states are kept defensively at bay, e.g., 'Parent contamination' could be when a client holds on to a belief which is clearly a message from their parent which they have swallowed whole, such as 'it's weak to cry'. 'Excluding Child' could be when a client is acting impulsively and egocentrically without using their Parent ability to nurture and set boundaries for themself or their Adult ability to recognise reality.

Health, in simple transactional analysis terms, is when the Adult has integrated the natural Child and the nurturing Parent but is not ruled by the adapted Child or the harsh Parent. This is very close to a co-dependency counsellor's understanding of health.

OTHER WORK

The above-mentioned theories all have links with co-dependency theory. In addition, individual psychoanalysts and therapists can add to our understanding of the theory and offer us pointers for practice, particularly in terms of understanding the damage caused by substituting our false self for our real self.

Dr Alice Miller writes convincingly about the true self's solitary confinement within the prison of the false self and also about how parents with unmet needs turn to their children to provide them, at the cost of the child's creativity, spontaneity and authenticity. She defines depression in terms of the loss of self and the denial of true feelings which begin as the child adapts to the parents' expectations. Hope lies in this person finding at least one adult who will tell them they are not to blame, and herein lies the counsellor's role – to support and to believe. Alice Miller believes that the violence in society has its roots in the violence prevalent in much child-rearing and emphasises the implications for parenting and education today.

Miller was following on from D. W. Winnicott, whose work with mothers and children showed him how often a child accommodates a parent's needs at the expense of their natural childlike narcissism. Winnicott saw that the true self is not easy to bring out, because it remains undeveloped and therefore does not know how to communicate. Co-dependency counsellors often witness the immaturity of their client's true self as it begins to emerge when an addiction loses its hold.

Carl Jung had also discovered the 'eternal child' amongst his clients, and believed that this child trapped within the adult could prevent individuation just as much as the over-controlling tendencies he saw in people.

Carl Rogers had his own terms for the loss of self. He described the creation of disturbance when a child's self-concept becomes out of touch with what he called the 'organismic self'. The organismic self becomes hidden and private when this self-concept is based on approval-seeking and avoidance of hostility.

Rogers' use of genuineness, empathy and unconditional positive regard was designed to enable the counsellor to show that he accepted the client fully and to therefore encourage complete self-acceptance. This method is useful in counselling co-dependent clients, especially as their immature but true self emerges and they feel the original shame of who they really are.

Having looked at some of the interlinking theories, Chapter 2 turns to how and when co-dependency theory and practice can be used when working with addictions.

2

Counselling the Addict

I imagine that when you read the title of this chapter you may well have imagined yourself sitting opposite a client addicted to heroin, or cocaine. Maybe even tranquillisers. You may have been in such a position and feel you can relate to this chapter. You may have never worked with a drug addict and be ready to dismiss this chapter as irrelevant to your work. Hang on. The first step towards an understanding of co-dependency is to throw away our narrow definitions of addiction. Picture instead a client who abuses drink. A client who is a compulsive overeater. A client who gambles their wages away on the first day of receiving them. These clients are also addicts. They may still fit your definition fairly easily. Let's take it a step further. Rachel knows smoking is ruining her health and her husband is forever asking her to stop, at least for the children's sake. She keeps smoking. Dunstan spends an inordinate amount of time shopping. He doesn't use or want half the things he buys and often spends more than he can afford. Mary has sex with everyone she goes on a date with and she doesn't insist they use contraception. She feels ashamed afterwards and worries that she is HIV positive. These feelings don't change her behaviour. Mahala works late every night and takes work home at weekends. Her friends have gradually left her because she is never available and she complains of loneliness. Dee always watches TV when her girlfriend comes round. The relationship is on the rocks.

When someone uses any substance, behaviour or process to the extent that it takes precedence over other priorities, yet cannot stop, despite an awareness of its increasingly harmful effects on their emotional or physical well-being, they are addicted. The addiction keeps the person out of touch with reality, and the need to remain out of touch with reality takes priority.

We are familiar with the consequences of the better-known addictions, for instance drink or drugs. These may include isolation, break-up of a marriage, imprisonment and even death. The consequences of less acknowledged addictions can be just as serious.

Moreover, whilst society frowns on the heroin addict, it is likely to reward the work addict with overtime cheques, to cheer on the compulsively sexual man or to romanticise the woman who is 'hopelessly in love' with a distant or abusive partner. Yet the work addict may die from stress-related heart disease; the sex addict may suffer from a sexual disease; the love addict may be beaten up or stay in a relationship where her children are abused.

I think that this wider definition has implications for counsellors. An awareness and an openness to the possibility of an addiction being present should always inform your practice, as there will be little progress if you are counselling your client about their marital difficulties whilst they are in denial about having compulsive sexual affairs outside the marriage. Equally your client may usefully talk to you about his memories of being beaten as a child and then go home and raid the fridge before the associated feelings have a chance to surface.

THEORIES OF ADDICTION

There continues to be much controversy over the theory of addiction and what causes people to become addicts. Addiction has been seen as a psychological disorder and attempts have been made to describe personality types who are more susceptible to becoming addicts. Addiction has been seen as the result of a socially acceptable escape route from problems, as in the use of sedatives to solve insomnia, or as a socially acceptable way to enjoy oneself, as in alcohol, or to expand one's mind in certain cultures, as in the use of LSD or opium. Family systems theory has also played a major part in the understanding and treatment of addiction. It treats the whole family rather than just the addict, seeing that they all need help to break out of unhealthy and rigid roles within the family, if the addiction is to be halted.

The concept of co-dependency evolved from understanding addiction as an organising principle in maintaining an unhealthy family system. This has been particularly useful in understanding eating disorders such as anorexia. Other theories have suggested that a person's genetic make-up may mean they will react differently to alcohol and are more likely to become an alcoholic.

A theory which links nature to nurture suggests that the addictive substance or behaviour releases certain internal brain chemicals. The different chemicals can cause feelings of comfort, excitement or control. Depending on the person's particular emotional need they become dependent upon the release of one of these brain chemicals. Repeating the addiction produces the release, and the sought-after feeling.

CO-DEPENDENCY AND ADDICTION

The link between co-dependency and addiction can be understood in two ways. First, a co-dependent person is likely to have an addiction, which they will use to mask the painful feelings of co-dependency. The addiction could be to a substance, a behaviour or another person. The painful feelings stem largely from a sense of shame about one's true self, resulting in a perceived need to present a false self.

Secondly, an addict will invariably show signs of co-dependency, which become more obvious both to them and you, once they stop their addiction. Your client may present you first with their addiction or with their co-dependency.

In my experience as a counsellor I have found that co-dependent clients, as well as having different addictions, have a need for a different emotional response. This can often be traced back to an unmet childhood need or a particular childhood pain which they are still medicating through their addiction. John, who was physically abused by both his father and mother and who describes home as a place of chaos, uses work as a means to gain control, achievement and perfection. Aisha, who was physically provided for as a child but never felt wanted or loved by her mother, overeats as a way of comforting herself.

In working with your client you may find that an awareness of their particular emotional need as outlined above points you to their as yet unacknowledged addictions. Conversely, working with your client on moving away from their addiction, you can help them to discover both the cause of their need for excitement/comfort/control and other healthier means to meet that need.

For co-dependents, the reality they are ultimately trying to avoid through addiction is the reality of their co-dependency, or loss of their real self. This is a vicious circle. Continuing the addiction halts the discovery of self. The client remains in a suspended state of maturity. Attending to their addiction takes priority over relating to others, and may seem a safer substitute. When they feel lonely or ashamed, rather than reach out, the addict turns to the addiction. How then can we as counsellors reach out to our clients? Let's not be too pessimistic. The fact that they are sitting in front of you is an enormous first step. Whether they have acknowledged their addiction or not, they are seeking counselling presumably because 'all is not right'.

However, we cannot help our clients look at their underlying co-dependency if they are using their addiction to such an extent that they are out of touch with reality. Pia Mellody names the addictions with this potential as: alcohol or drug addiction; sex addiction (depending on severity); gambling (depending on severity); and severe eating disorders (e.g. at life-threatening stage), and suggests that the client must first achieve a degree of sobriety from these addictions before any further work can be done (Mellody, Workshop for Professionals, London, November 1991).

However, other less reality-destroying addictions, or more moderate forms of the afore-mentioned addictions do not need to be addressed first and the client may well not be willing to give them up until some healing and ability to gain internal comfort has been achieved. If this is the case for your client, the main task is to ensure that he at least practises his addiction in full awareness. If you are counselling your client and he is talking about the emotional neglect in his family of origin he may be overeating between sessions as the painful feelings surface. He may start smoking again. It is important that as a counsellor you encourage him to tell you, rather than hide the

10

fact, and that you convey a non-judgemental but not collusive response. As he begins to use his addiction 'in awareness' he realises for example that when he feels distress, he overeats, or that when he feels angry, he lights up a cigarette. This awareness can be facilitated by using a diary, which he shares with you at some point during the counselling session. This method hinders denial, which is a major part of addiction.

LOVE ADDICTION

I want to look at this addiction separately as it is often subject to confusion and controversy. There is a resistance to describing a person who persistently chooses inappropriate partners and has difficulty ending unhealthy relationships as a love addict. Perhaps it is due to acceptance by society that, for women at least, an addiction to love is desirable and normal. Another complaint is that the pathology focuses upon the woman for staying in an abusive relationship rather than on the man's abuse of power. The theory is indeed damaging if it serves to indemnify male violence. However, looking at why a woman may be drawn to abusive relationships does not in my opinion close the door on challenging men who are violent. It is as important to find ways of empowering the oppressed as it is to confront the oppressor. If you are working with a woman in this situation, seeing her as addicted offers new ways of helping her to free herself. I should add that love addicts can be men, although it is less common.

The characteristics of love addiction are similar to those of any substance addiction. For example, making the other person more important than any other priority, fantasising about them when not with them, believing that being with them will solve all other problems. As it intensifies, obsessing about the other person, denying the reality of the relationship as harmful consequences emerge, feeling unable to extricate oneself as the fantasy crumbles, becoming secretive to hide the shame associated with being in this relationship.

Love addiction has been confused with co-dependency. It is not the same thing. It is simply another addiction used to cover up the pain of co-dependency. Many counsellors work with love addicts, thinking that their role is to focus on the relationship, either to help heal it, or to encourage the client

11

to leave it. This is not useful. Until the client addresses her co-dependency issues, particularly those of self-image and self-care, she will continue to stay in unhealthy relationships.

THE ROLE OF SHAME

Another useful approach to understanding addiction is in the context of shame. Deep internalised shame is the result of not being valued for who we are. It is the result of hiding our true self as we grew up. It is different from healthy shame. Healthy shame is a feeling we all have from time to time which serves to remind us that we are not perfect. For example, I say that I will ring a friend on Monday evening and I put it off until Friday evening. Come Friday my friend tells me that she sat in waiting for my call all Monday because she really needed to talk to me. I realise I have no genuine excuse and feel shame. I am exposed as being less than the perfect friend. This is healthy because it stops me from becoming arrogant. I am reminded that my actions can hurt others, even if it is unintentional. However, in recognising that I have behaved as an imperfect friend I will not conclude that I am therefore a useless person if I have a healthy core inside me which says 'I'm still basically ok when I make a mistake'. Such a healthy core develops naturally if we are brought up with this message from our original caregivers.

Unhealthy shame, sometimes called toxic shame, occurs when a person feels that their very self is imperfect and therefore unlovable and of no value. When they make a mistake or behave inappropriately the original sense of imperfection is triggered. Linking this to addiction and co-dependency explains the role of shame. A co-dependent person is full of shame, so much so that they have hidden their true self from others and from their own self. The pain of losing their true self and the conflict felt as the true self continuously attempts to resurface can be suppressed by the addictive process, whereby the focus is exclusively on the addiction.

However at some level the client is aware that each time he indulges his addiction he is behaving 'less than perfectly'. This triggers the original shame and intensifies the need to suppress the feelings of shame.

Working with an addict, the counsellor must therefore aim

Counselling the addict

at removing the layers of shame, top layer first. This means first removing the shame about the addiction. As society often disapproves of certain addictions it is essential for the counsellor to check out her own reactions to and beliefs about addictions, to ensure that she can work with an addict in a non-judgemental way.

Figure 1 (p. 14) is an example of how shame can fuel an addiction, in this case, love addiction, and how the counsellor can most usefully work in such a case. The client is a love addict, who feels unable to leave an unhappy relationship.

The counsellor in this case can help to remove the feeling of shame and thus stop fuelling the addictive process. Providing the woman is not in immediate physical danger the counsellor gives her client permission not to make the decision to leave for now. She provides her client with information about her addiction and co-dependency and encourages her to take the focus off the relationship and her partner for the moment.

At first the counsellor may well find that her client does not want to switch focus. In using the session to talk about her partner and the relationship with him the client is indulging her addiction. However she may also feel a great sense of relief at being told she does not have to make a decision she feels incapable of making. Also, through realising that it is an addiction she can understand why it is so hard to break away from it. It is not because she is useless. She need not feel shame.

Critics of the concept of addiction and powerlessness argue that it keeps the client in victim role. I would argue that its purpose is to remove stigmatisation. If the addict assumes she is responsible for her addiction she reinforces those initial feelings of shame: 'I am useless to the core.' She can mask the shame by continuing the addiction. The premise that the addict did not choose to become an addict and feels powerless over her addiction does not preclude the ability to recover from that state. The client is relieved of shame for the original addiction and handed back responsibility for future recovery.

CONTROL

One of the triggers of shame in addiction is the client's attempt to remain in control of it. Perhaps for some addicts control can work, but if they are using their addiction to mask their

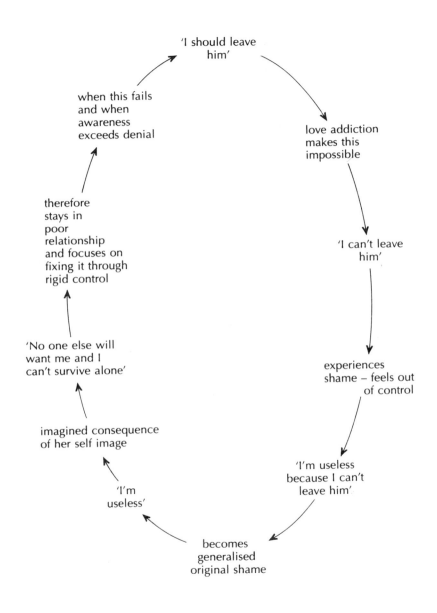

Figure 1 How shame feeds addiction

14

Counselling the addict

co-dependency, i.e., their feelings of shame about who they are, the need to continue the addiction is usually greater than the ability to control it. Failure to control can cause the addict to feel even more shame.

Addictions are either about being out of control, rigidly in control or switching from one to the other. The need to control stems from powerlessness and fear. *NB*

Anorexics starve themselves and get their 'high' from controlling their food intake and their quest for a perfect body. They lose control of reality when they see their body as fat when it is in fact thin. Bulimics binge until their eating is out of control. They then control the outcome by vomiting or abusing laxatives. Workaholics often need to control the work around them and will not delegate what is quite properly someone else's task.

On a lower level are behaviours such as the need to wash one's hands constantly or feeling unable to relax unless the house is always tidy. Charlotte Kasl describes how many of her clients recalled that compulsive behaviour began whilst they were being abused – they would count or recall a repetitive pattern of thoughts to disassociate from, and thereby control, reality (Kasl 1990: 30). Compulsions can be manageable or unmanageable. When they are unmanageable they are addictions.

To be addicted is to be out of control. When a sex addict has sex with a stranger he didn't mean to have sex with, he is out of control. When a compulsive overeater eats four chocolate bars in a row despite knowing it will make him sick like last time, he is out of control. When an alcoholic drinks another bottle of wine despite already being drunk, she is out of control. The addict is using their addiction to try and control their feelings. Paradoxically the controlling impulse is so strong that the addiction becomes out of control.

As a counsellor working with an addict, it helps to be aware of the issues around control. It is beneficial to the client if you can enable them to let go of control in the counselling session, perhaps just for two or three minutes. You might try a relaxation exercise. If a client controls through talking, you might stop them mid-sentence and ask what happens if they are silent. You might suggest they do something (safe) they wouldn't normally do in a session, such as run around the

15

room, throw cushions. Explore what being 'out of control' and 'in control' means to them. Educate your client about addiction and the impossibility of controlling an addiction simply by using enough willpower. Encourage your client to seek a self-help group and if necessary look at how being 'in control' for them may be equated with going it alone. Look at the harmful consequences of being 'out of control' of the addiction.

DENIAL

One of the hardest obstacles to tackling addiction is denial, an integral part of addiction. It could be that your client denies they are addicted or that there is a problem. It could be that they accept they have an addiction but deny its consequences for themselves or others.

Denial occurs when we do not want to admit reality. Denial within addiction occurs when the client is faced with the conflict of addiction. If he faces up to the reality that he is an addict, that label may involve stigma. It may also mean he has to face the fact that he is harming himself and others, and not dealing with other pressing needs in his life. Above all, however, if he accepts he has an addiction, he will feel the pressure that he then has a choice to remove the addiction. The addiction is however, his greatest priority, as his means to avoid feelings of discomfort. It is far easier to continue to deny there is a problem and feel free to pursue his addiction.

In order to deny, he may become secretive. He may lie; he may isolate; he may blame others, including his counsellor; he may insist it is within his control. His partner or family are likely to collude with his denial and I will deal with this in the next chapter. You, as a counsellor, may also be tempted to collude if it is painful for you to acknowledge your client's unmanageable life, or if you too are denying an addiction of your own.

Helping your client break through denial does not involve you taking on responsibility for your client. Your part is to offer to discuss addiction with him, and to let him know that you are there to help him make changes if and when he is ready. Your part is to make it permissible to talk about addiction by making an assumption that any of your clients may have addictions. One way to communicate this message is to have some relevant leaflets available in your consultation room. Another way is to include your philosophy of addiction when introducing how you work in your initial session. Don't worry if your client does not respond at this point. The important point is that you have put it on the agenda and communicated your non-judgemental approach. This may well set your session aside as different from the client's home or work environment, where the addiction is known, but not talked about, or where the client has been judged as a failure because of his addiction.

ACKNOWLEDGING HARMFUL CONSEQUENCES

When your client moves out of denial he has acknowledged his addiction to some extent. It may be simply a recognition such as 'Yes, I'm having trouble controlling my gambling', 'I drink too much' or 'I do tend to blow my money on shopping sprees, even when it means I go overdrawn'. At this point I want to clarify that the word addiction may be more useful to you, the counsellor, as a concept which informs your work, than to your client. Some people find it useful to call themselves a drug addict, an alcoholic, a sex addict, and some co-dependency counsellors prefer these terms as it can prevent denial of the problem, and can help the client feel they deserve help, rather than that they are a failure. Others find the word sticks in their throat, given its negative connotations and the suggestion that the person's personality is limited to being an addict. Critics of co-dependency theory would agree. I do not think it matters and I would not try to use the word with someone who found it added to their sense of shame. It's important for the client to come to self-definition and for many, *choosing* to call themselves an addict or their problem an addiction makes a transition in their own definition of the problem. Kasl identifies this dilemma as arising when you mistake your labels for your identity (Kasl 1990: 34). If your client names himself as an addict it is important to explore with him what that means and to accept his definition. However at some point, in a later session, encourage him to find other descriptions of himself, positive and negative, so that he sees that 'addict' is just one thing he is. If he shuns the words addiction and addict do the same exercise and ask him if it would then be easier to add addict to the list.

Acknowledging harmful consequences is best done using writing work. Putting words on paper makes the talked-about events more concrete and means they do not disappear after the session. The client can take his notes with him, maybe with the suggestion that he adds to them if new thoughts occur. There are many ways to approach this work. My suggestion for headings to write under would be: Harmful consequences to my (1) physical health, (2) mental health, (3) emotional health, (4) finances, (5) relationships with friends, (6) relationships with partner, (7) family, (8) work, (9) leisure. You may add others if they seem relevant to your client, or you may do so in consultation with your client.

If this is too overwhelming for your client, they may prefer to look at consequences of a particular week. This exercise can be very painful for your client as the reality surfaces. They will feel shame at exposing the consequences of their addiction to you. It should be done slowly. Acceptance on your part is essential, and demonstrating Carl Rogers' unconditional positive regard is a skill particularly useful for working with shame-filled people. Supervision may be needed to clarify your own values at this time, as if they are contradicted by what your client tells you you may find your acceptance has limitations or is not genuine. Your client may throw your acceptance back at you, i.e., 'only a ridiculous person could still value me after all I've just told you'. Your maturity is called upon to see the shame behind this personal rejection. Your client may also retreat still further into their addiction at this stage.

If your client does turn more to their addiction, or refuses to move out of denial even when the extent of the harm is becoming clear to you, what will you do?

It is important at this stage, for both your client's and your own well-being, that you learn to 'let go'. You may find this relatively easy in comparison to the client's partner or family. However, a good many counsellors are compulsive caretakers who yearn to 'fix' their clients and feel they have failed if they cannot 'fix' them. Below are some responses to beware or be aware of when you are counselling an addict:

Counselling the addict

1 *Anger and blame.* Do you feel that their refusal to face their addiction reflects badly on you?
2 *Collusion.* Is it easier to join your client in believing there is not a problem? Do you fear they will dislike you if you confront them?
3 *Loss of control.* True. You have no control over your client's addiction. He will give up when he is ready, no sooner.
4 *Responsibility.* You are not responsible for the addict, only for being available to help if and when they face up to *their* responsibility.
5 *Loss.* Letting go involves letting go of the belief that you can change them. Letting go brings up feelings of loss and its attendant emotions, e.g. grief, anger.

DECISION TO QUIT

Your client has decided to stop drinking, using cocaine, over-spending, overeating, smoking. The debate between controlling addiction and total abstinence continues to be argued, and I do not intend to address it here. I am assuming that stopping means abstinence because your client has been unable to control their addiction. Of course, it is impossible to achieve total abstinence from eating, spending money and for most people, sex. It is therefore important that your client reaches their own definition of 'sobriety' and that you do not impose your definition.

Example 1: Overeating

No sugar, no chocolate, no McDonalds! No cappucino, only three meals a day, no snacks in between. Not going to café after evening class on Tuesday. Drink less when I go out to dinner as I overeat when I drink too much.

Example 2: Love addiction

Two people's 'sobriety' could be very different.

Pete: End relationship with Jane. No relationships for at least one year. After a year go out with lots of women on casual dates and don't fall for first woman I meet.

Gary: Stop talking about Mark in therapy. Stop trying to change Mark. See friends at least two times per week. Get full-time job so not financially dependent on Mark. Stop buying clothes Mark likes and start dressing to please me.

At this stage your client needs maximum support, and should be encouraged to reach out for whatever help is available. For some addictions they may need a period of in-patient treatment and they will certainly need medical supervision if they are to come off tranquillisers. As a counsellor you should have available a list of resources in your area.

GROUP AND FAMILY SUPPORT

I have found that group support is invaluable to the person attempting to stay stopped. Stopping itself is not necessarily a problem. The courage not to go back to the addiction is where the struggle lies and it may take your client many attempts and many relapses along the way. Twelve-step groups are self-help groups modelled on Alcoholics Anonymous and are available throughout the country. They are called '12-step groups' because they follow a programme which advocates twelve stages believed to be necessary for recovery. These stages include accepting the unmanageability of life with an addiction, looking to spiritual support to overcome the addiction and facing the reality of how the addiction has affected others. There are peer support groups for various addictions which are open to anyone who acknowledges they have a problem and wants to stop their particular addiction. They have a spiritual approach which is non-denominational. Their strength is that they are free, and frequent, and if necessary members will provide daily support for each other. I would recommend that you have a list available of 12-step groups in your area. Your client may not choose to use this form of support, and there are other self-help or support groups which may suit them better. The point I am making is that your client needs to break out of the self-imposed isolation which usually accompanies an addiction and is shame-based, which means they feel unable to say 'I need help' or 'I have a problem'.

You may choose to set up a group yourself, or encourage

your client to do so. A group for recovering addicts must, in my opinion, have several key factors which link to the concepts I have described in this chapter.

1 It must be non-judgemental regarding addiction.
2 It must be non-collusive regarding addiction.
3 It must be accepting to the point that each person can be themselves and not be shamed for it.
4 If it is a led group the leader should be democratic and willing to appropriately self-disclose.
5 The group leader should model imperfection and flexibility as healthy and desirable.
6 The group leader should desist from being the answer-provider, even under pressure from the group.
7 Ideally there should be members with some experience of abstinence/sobriety. They can offer hope to the newer members and in turn be helped to avoid complacency (which can lead to relapse) by hearing newer members' struggles.
8 The group should be for one addiction only, to avoid false hierarchies of addiction, e.g. 'staying away from certain foods isn't as hard as staying off heroin'. Although under-lying difficulties are often revealed to be remarkably simi-lar, these unhelpful hierarchies often persist, especially in early recovery.
9 All emotions must be allowed, including the safe expression of anger. Relapse often occurs when anger sur-faces and is repressed.
10 Anxiety reduction should be addressed, e.g. breathing exercises, relaxation techniques. Anxiety and panic attacks can surface when an addiction is halted and clients need to learn healthy strategies to manage this.

The counsellor needs to be aware that addiction is often a family problem. If the client is still connected to his or her family the changes they make will have repercussions within the family. The same can apply with a partner. I examine this in more detail in the next chapter. A counsellor may be distressed to hear of the family/partner's attempts to sabotage their client's recovery. This is common if the other significant members of that client's system are not helped in their own right, through counselling, family therapy or self-help groups, whether 12-step groups such as Al-Anon or other suitable groups. You can help your client by educating him about the role others play in his addiction. It may be that for a time he needs to cut himself off from these people if they present a real threat to his recovery. Counselling will help him make this decision.

RELAPSE

Relapses can and often do happen. If you are counselling your client regularly there should be danger signals – relapse rarely happens out of the blue. You can help by encouraging your client to recognise his danger signals, e.g. a sober gambler starts to buy the *Racing Post* 'just to browse through', a sex addict returns to the club where he used to pick up women 'just for a dance'. These signals should ring alarm bells that the client is not paying attention and care to his sobriety. Of course, as a counsellor, you can only work with your client if he feels able to confide his danger signals to you. If he keeps them secret he is on the road to shame and denial and probable relapse. The best approach is to discuss the possibility as early on as you can, to indicate that you know relapse can happen and that you will not think badly of the client if it does. Encourage him to share the danger signals, but if in doing so it becomes clear that relapse is imminent and inevitable it may be time to let go again. Don't despair. Instead, invite your client to relapse in full awareness, i.e., to check out his feelings before, during and after. Your client may be furious with you for encouraging him to act in full awareness because it removes the addictive high. However if he can do so, and returns to you with a full report of what happened for him, the relapse has more chance of being short-lived and he will have moved on.

THE NEXT STEP

Finally, when sobriety has been maintained for a considerable period, the counsellor may begin co-dependency work. This should not be started too early. It may need to wait a whole year after the client has halted his addiction. Looking at childhood trauma can be too unsettling for someone beginning sobriety and can lead to relapse. However, it should also not be neglected. Treatment that deals solely with the addiction and not with the underlying co-dependency is rarely successful in the long term. A sober alcoholic may become what is called a 'dry drunk', as their repressed and shamed anger surfaces in the form of rage. A love addict may abstain from unhealthy relationships but experience overwhelming depression as his underlying feelings of abandonment emerge. Your client may well at this stage simply swap addictions. I have seen many ex-heroin addicts turn to drink, and many ex-love addicts become overeaters. The issues of co-dependency I describe in Chapters 4 and 5 need addressing if your client's recovery is to be whole.

DISCUSSION ISSUES

1 Do you feel differently about a heroin addict, someone addicted to tranquillisers, an overeater? How do you feel differently and why? Which addictions are you most judge-mental about?

2 What do you do to avoid painful reality? Is it compulsive/ an addiction?

3 What is the effect of self-imposed isolation on an addict?

4 Think of times you have had to 'let go' of a person or situation. How have you dealt with it?

5 Compare the value of one-to-one counselling versus group counselling for an addict.

3

Co-dependency and Addiction

Counselling the partner

As counsellors, we may often find ourselves counselling the partner of an addict. The partner may come to us directly with this problem, or it may arise if we are counselling him or her about an unsatisfactory relationship and the issue of their partner's addiction becomes clear as a contributory factor. Through understanding co-dependency, I am always alerted if my client talks continuously about her partner, even if there is no mention of addiction. Someone who is 'hooked' on their partner and on changing their partner may well be in a relationship with an addict.

This is the original meaning of co-dependency. Professionals working in alcohol and drug treatment centres experienced their client's recovery whilst these people remained at the centres. However, on their return to families or partners, clients often relapsed. Addiction began to be understood as a family 'dis-ease'. It was as if the family or partner were dependent on the client remaining addicted in order to keep the focus on the client as the one with a problem. Often partners held the belief that if they were perfect, the client's addiction would be solved, and that as, in spite of all their efforts, the client could or would not end their addiction, they were therefore imperfect. Underneath this desire to be the perfect care-takers, there was often a heap of supressed anger. Often the anger surfaced only when the addict achieved abstinence. Partners of addicts were often also seen to tolerate extremely abusive situations resulting from the client's addiction, ranging from violence to bankruptcy to abuse of their children, yet seemed unable to leave the relationship, just as the client was unable to put down the substance.

Counselling the partner

Counsellors working with partners of addicts also described how these partners, whilst knowing so much about the addict, showed little self-awareness or ability to look after their own needs.

Co-dependents of addicted clients began to be recognised, but it took time for them to be helped and seen as needing counselling in their own right, not just as an extension of the addict.

If this form of co-dependency is seen as a response to the pain of living with an addict it can be understood as part of the system which operates when addiction is present. For example:

1   An addict often lies – the partner begins to become watchful and mistrustful.
2   An addict's life is often out of control – the partner begins to overcontrol to compensate.
3   An addict can be irresponsible – the partner takes on all the responsibility.
4   An addict can be self-centred – the partner loses sense of herself.
5   An addict's world is often chaotic as everything, such as health, relationships, finances, takes second place to the addiction. The partner's world, bound up with his, also begins to lose sense and rationality.

Addicts may use their partner's excessive controlling or care-taking as a reason to continue their addiction. John commented: 'She's always watching over me, just waiting for me to make a slip. I feel like going out and using just to say to her – there you are then, happy now?' Counsellors may even collude with this: 'You can understand why he drinks, having to put up with her constant nagging and fussing.' Co-dependents are no more to blame for their obsession than addicts are to blame for their addiction – both need help. If we help the co-dependent to begin to take care of themself and assume responsibility for their own happiness, it often happens that the addicted partner also makes a shift and begins to take responsibility for their recovery. It doesn't always happen. That person may continue to drink, use drugs, overeat, gamble. Nevertheless, the co-dependent's happiness need no longer be dependent on the behaviour of the addict. She will either find a way to live more happily alongside the addict, or she may decide that she no longer wishes that person to be a part of her life. As a counsellor it is important to clarify with your client that you are *not* working with her: (1) to help her 'fix' her partner; (2) to persuade her to leave her partner. Exceptions to (2) may exist if you have concerns that she is at physical risk, or that her children are at physical risk. How you work with these issues will depend on a number of factors, including if you are working for an agency with statutory obligations and your own ethical practice. I do not intend to cover this here, but it is obviously important that you are clear about your position or your agency's position before you begin counselling.

FOCUSING CLIENT ON SELF

I am assuming that you have reached a stage in counselling your client whereby she has acknowledged that her partner has an addiction. It is quite likely that your client will initially talk about her partner more than herself. This is necessary at the beginning. She may have felt too ashamed to share her problem with others and this could be the first time she has told anyone. The burden of secrecy will be greatly relieved by sharing with you. Alternately, she may have talked about it so much with other people that they are sick of listening to her or have begun to question why she puts up with a partner whose life is in such chaos. As her counsellor, your non-judgemental ear will be valued. As she tells you about the consequences of her partner's inappropriate behaviours you may feel distressed or enraged, and wonder where your client's anger has disappeared to. Or you may find that her anger, often taking the form of complaining and martyrdom, leaves you too wondering why she puts up with this life.

Your role is to find the right time to gently point out that your client has talked about her partner for long enough and that you now want to switch the focus onto her. She may resist, and until she is ready to look at herself your task remains to face her with this fact. If this persists for too long you will find it useful to be more challenging. Point out the 'victim role' behind your client's statements. If she begins to relate another 'listen to what he did last week' story, ask your client to clarify what they feel about what 'he' did and to work with you on what they can do about dealing with what he did.

Ultimately you may need to be more upfront. For example: 'I am not here to help you to fix your partner'; 'I am not here to listen to you tell me how bad it is each week but to help you work out how you want to proceed'; 'I really don't think I can help you if you continue to spend the sessions focusing on your partner'.

As your client begins to focus on herself it may come to light that she doesn't know what she thinks or feels. *Her* feelings and thoughts have been neglected for so long in deference to his, that she has lost all sense of self. Or she doesn't believe anyone is truly interested in what she feels, particularly if her partner has been receiving help or treatment. As the focus continues to be on her she will gain confidence in her renewed sense of self. If your client's co-dependency is more deeply rooted, as is often the case, in a loss of self from early years, you may need to teach the basic emotions. I cover this in Chapter 5.

As counselling progresses, she may slip back into focusing on her partner, out of habit, or when the focus on herself is too painful. A reminder should be more readily received at this stage, if she does not recognise what she is doing herself.

FOUR ROLES TO WATCH FOR

Your client may fall into one of these four roles, and may switch, particularly between rescuer, controller and victim. The joiner who adopts her partner's addiction is less common but I have seen it happen. It is useful to identify these roles with your client and point out when you see your client moving into them, or stuck in them. Look at what lies underneath the role.

Rescuer

I am indispensable. I can save you. Let me take care of you. I can anticipate your needs even before you do, even when you don't. You are a helpless victim.

Underneath: I only feel important when I am helping.

Controller

Let me sort your life out. Put your life in my hands. I know what's best for you. Here's some good advice.

Underneath: I only feel powerful when you are dependent on me. I am terrified of my dependence on you.

Victim

Why me? What have I done to deserve this? Poor me. This always happens to me whatever I do. It's pointless trying to change things.

Underneath: I only feel happy when I am suffering.

Joiner

Don't leave me. Don't be different. See how much I love you. What's good for you is good enough for me.

Underneath: Who I am is not important – I exist to please you.

The transactional analysis tool 'the Karpman triangle' is also useful in looking at and undoing these roles and I will discuss this in Chapter 5.

DENIAL AND COLLUSION

Although your client has acknowledged the problem, she may still be in denial as to the effect it is having on her life. She may tell a story of her partner's addictive behaviour and its consequences and then find excuses for them:

He got drunk at the party and flirted with all his business colleagues and then began telling stories about our private life. . . . He only did it because he's feeling insecure about our relationship.

Sometimes she blames herself:

He came home and told me he'd used cocaine last night. I shouted at him before he went out and didn't apologise even though I knew I was in the wrong.

28

They may minimise the problem to you and others out of shame – the partner's addiction has become your client's shame. Or they may minimise it to themselves because the pain of facing the extent of their partner's addiction is so great and because they may see it as proof that their partner does not love them. Denial can be easily challenged once your client is open about what is happening in her life. Encourage your client to relate the history of her partner's addiction with reference to the harmful consequences for herself. This can be done verbally or in written form. Ask her to pinpoint when she began to deny the reality of the addiction by minimising or rationalising its effects, and also when she began to develop an increasing tolerance towards her partner's addictive behaviour.

Be aware that as you counsel your client through and out of the denial stage she may feel overwhelmed by the reality of her powerlessness over her partner. Her controlling behaviour may increase as she makes a last-ditch attempt to 'fix' her partner rather than accept reality. She may return to you in emotional turmoil relating her attempts such as a threat to leave unless he stops (this threat is rarely carried through and therefore soon loses its power). More likely he will continue his addiction in spite of the threat and she will feel the despair that not even their relationship means more to him than his addiction.

BLAME AND SHAME

The co-dependent often searches for someone to blame for her partner's addiction, as a way of making sense of the condition. This is often seen in families when parents of an addict blame each other. She says the father was too soft on his son, he says the mother didn't spend enough time with her son. Or they both say that their other son was too demanding or too clever or too sacrificing and made their addicted son feel left out, unintelligent, act selfishly. As I mentioned earlier, the addict will play on this as it helps take away from his own feelings of shame, and gives him a reason to continue his addiction. Counselling the partner, you may often hear her blame the addict's family – for not understanding him, or his friends for leading him into it in the first place. It is easier for your client to blame 'outsiders' than to express the anger she feels towards her partner or the shame she feels at herself for failing. This will alternate with blaming the partner and blaming herself. Clients need reassurance that they are not to blame for their partner's addiction, that it did not start as a result of anything they had done or not done, and that there is no guarantee that anything they do or don't do will cause their partner to stop. The partner is not abusing alcohol because he does not love your client, he is abusing it because he has an addiction to it.

Blaming the partner often occurs when your client has attempted to rescue her partner, often totally inappropriately. She is likely to have treated her partner as a victim who is incapable of taking responsibility for his actions. For example, Susan who always pays for her partner's court fines when he commits criminal acts through alcohol abuse; Stephen who rings up his partner's work to tell lies about her having to attend a funeral, when she is away from home trying to buy drugs.

Your client is trying to protect her partner from reality under the illusion that if life becomes any more difficult for him he may crack under the strain and turn more to the addiction. Or because she thinks that if he sees how much she loves him and is willing to help him out of a sticky situation he will give up his addiction out of gratitude. Or perhaps it is in some way an act of martyrdom in itself: 'See how much I sort out your problems, see how indispensable I am, see how much you put me through.' None of these achieve the desired result. The partner is saved from facing the consequences of his addiction and is enabled to continue. The client then feels used and abused and furious and begins to blame.

Point out to your client that she is blaming because he will not let her 'helping' control his life and that her helping is in fact hindering. Your client needs support and reassurance to stop helping unhelpfully. It takes courage to step back and allow someone to face painful consequences, such as loss of a job, arrest, exposure. It is particularly hard if your client will also suffer from those consequences. But she is doubtlessly suffering already.

Shame often lies beneath the blame. Co-dependents often have poor internal boundaries. By this I mean that they are confused as to where their feelings begin and those of their partner end. They therefore feel that their partner's addiction and the behaviour caused by the addiction is *their* shame, taking responsibility for what is undoubtedly their partner's repressed feeling. If someone else's behaviour causes you to feel shame, then you will have a big investment in controlling their behaviour, as is common in partners of addicts. As a counsellor, your role is to help your client identify what it is about her partner's behaviour which causes her to feel shame. You can then begin to encourage her to look at other responses she could have. This concept of choice about how she feels may surprise your client, but can prove liberating. Going deeper with your client at this stage may reveal that this burden of feeling another person's feelings (especially if that person is in denial of those feelings) often stems from childhood. Your client may need to grieve the responsibility that was placed upon them as a child by an adult caregiver, for that adult's emotional pain and problems. Work on strengthening inner boundaries to separate one person's feelings from another's is also useful and I will discuss this in Chapter 5.

SELF-ESTEEM

Whilst your client continues to feel responsibility for and shame about their partner's addiction, their self-esteem will continue to plummet. Because they cannot control the addiction they will falsely assume that they are useless, and that it is all 'their fault'. This free-flowing low self-esteem often causes the partner to isolate. She may cut off from her family because she senses she is seen as a failure for being involved with an addict. Of course the family may view her as such, if they too do not understand addiction, or if they have a vested interest in seeing your client as a failure. She may also cut off from her friends, believing that no one will understand the crazy world she lives in. If she does mix with them she may hide that part of her life, meaning she will not get the support she needs. Whilst your role can be crucial in alleviating some of the isolation, a group composed of others in the same situation is invaluable. A client may expect a degree of acceptance from you. 'That's your job' one client told me. They can then devalue your acceptance and continue to see themselves as unacceptable. Acceptance by a group of people who are not paid to listen or trained as counsellors can be harder to dismiss.

Advise your client to join a group which focuses strictly on the co-dependent's experiences and not on the addict, except insofar as they affect the partner.

The group should focus on solutions as well as on suffering, so that your client comes away not just relieved of painful feelings, but armed with strategies and hope. A valuable group can:

1 Relieve isolation and stigma. Everyone is 'in the same boat'.
2 Offer support during the group meeting and outside, through informal contacts.
3 Listen and not pass judgement.
4 Share experiences that offer hope and solutions.
5 For clients who have suppressed feelings, hearing someone else describe a situation they thought only they had suffered, with emotions, can release their own emotion.

Encourage your client to reach out and find a suitable group. If there is not one locally, they might set up their own self-help group. However, it may be some time before they join a group. It takes courage to 'go public' with your problem. Appropriate literature may help meanwhile, as there are a number of books written by partners of addicts and on co-dependency.

LETTING GO

When your client has worked through the stages of denial and blame and has accepted that they cannot fix their partner they may be ready to let go and begin to live their own lives. Letting go involves a grieving process as there is a loss for your client to mourn.

The loss will have individual significance for each client but can include:

1 Loss of what the partner or what the relationship could have been (loss of hopes and dreams).
2 Loss of respect for partner.
3 Loss of trust for partner.
4 Possibly loss of love for the partner.
5 Loss of security, be it physical, social, financial, emotional.
6 Loss of client's role as caretaker.

7   Loss of control.
8   Loss of self-image in relation to partner.

As a counsellor you may feel that your client has everything to gain by letting go, but the sense of gain may not be immediately apparent to the client, or may be their first feeling, to be replaced by grief as the euphoria of relief subsides. It is important that you facilitate the process of grieving and allow your client as much time as she needs for this process.

The experience of loss and grieving may be similar to suffering a bereavement. Here are some ways to help your client through this process.

(1) Help your client make the loss real and final. This involves encouraging your client to relate to you how he sees the loss in concrete terms. For co-dependents the main loss may be giving up on the dream of what could have been. Your client needs to see the loss as final so that they can then move on. Of course his partner may stop drinking, but this hope has kept him trapped in her life and unable to pursue his life for too long. For now, he needs to accept the fact of her addiction.

(2) Help your clients identify and express their feelings. Some may be easier than others, but for co-dependents there is often suppressed anger hidden beneath the ever-helpful caretaker. When your client begins to see that it may not be her fault that her partner is an addict she may move out of the victim role for the last time and for a period experience the opposite, persecutory feelings that go hand-in-hand. Fritz Perls said that underneath guilt lies resentment and this too may surface as your client 'lets go'. The anger may also stem from the intense fear and hurt of abandonment. Your client may not have been physically abandoned by her partner, but she may well have been emotionally abandoned in favour of the addiction. Encourage your client to express the anger with you and also to find a safe physical outlet, be it bodywork, massage or exercise. Other feelings which may surface include helplessness. Your client, so adept at looking after the addict, is likely to believe they truly cannot look after themselves. Letting go need not mean leaving their partner but it does involve beginning to be responsible for their own life. Your client may be fearful that they cannot do this. Your task is to reality-test this fear. It may involve negotiating with your client a set of

tasks that she has neglected whilst she has been obsessively trying to fix her partner. Thelma had neglected all responsibilities around her flat, whilst pursuing an unavailable sex addict partner. When she let go of him she began to face what needed doing. We spent a number of sessions working on her need to call in a surveyor to assess an internal damp problem. Whilst this woman had survived many abusive relationships and held down a demanding profession, her helplessness was almost overwhelming when she focused on her own needs before others. Not uncommonly, my client's helplessness betrayed a stubborn refusal to take care of herself, an angry response to her early family situation when no one had cared for her. Whilst deeper therapeutic work can release your client's hidden motives and help them grieve the pain which led them to become co-dependent in the first place, it is also useful for your client in the early stages of letting go to find coping strategies for tasks that maybe cannot wait.

ENCOURAGE YOUR CLIENT TO LIVE THEIR LIFE FULLY

As well as neglecting responsibilities, co-dependent clients may have neglected their own interests and hobbies, their friends, their career, other family members including children and their need for some fun! Your client needs support and encouragement to withdraw all that emotional energy from their partner and reinvest it for themselves. Ask your client to list all the things they have stopped doing that they used to enjoy, before they became caught up with their partner's addiction. She may have forgotten how to enjoy life and need to relearn. Advise her to try reinstigating one thing at a time. Part of meeting her own needs may also be to learn to ask for what she needs. This can involve asking individuals, or joining a group where her needs become known. Co-dependents are notoriously bad at this. Asking for help means saying 'I can't do this alone', thereby admitting vulnerability. It means losing control or power if someone else becomes involved in helping you, it means taking the risk of rejection if the person asked can or will not help. Your client has probably isolated herself for so long that reaching out to others will feel alien and frightening at first. She may even reach out to inappropriate people to prove her point that no one wants to help anyway.

For the client for whom letting go meant leaving her partner, living her life fully does not mean plunging straight into another relationship. Obviously you cannot prevent your client from doing so, but a discussion before it happens may alert the client to the possibility and the drawbacks, e.g. not mourning her previous partner, not learning to meet her own needs, or the risk of being drawn to another unavailable person if this is a pattern for her.

As mentioned previously, letting go need not involve separation. Neither does it involve being uncaring, although the client may complain that she *feels* she is being uncaring. She can still encourage any attempt her partner makes at halting his addiction, or seeking help to do so. She can still let him know that she values him, if not the part of him that is the addiction. Some counsellors call this 'detaching with love'. However, if it is not possible to detach with love, then encourage your client to detach anyway, even if it is in anger. Only then can your client begin to express and release her resentment so that she can go on to live her life more freely.

ABSTINENCE

Finally, how can you counsel your client if her partner achieves abstinence? What's the problem, you may ask, isn't that what she always wanted? Why should she need counselling now?

It is at this point that your client may really begin to feel and express her rage. It may only seem safe to do so now. Once the immediate pain and fear has subsided, the pain and fear accumulated over the past become apparent. All that she has tolerated for so long appears intolerable and she may rage that she did tolerate it.

In addition, particularly if your client was less successful in letting go, her familiar role may no longer be called for. What was so unpleasant was at least familiar. Now the partner who behaved so unreasonably and irresponsibly is coping without the addiction. The client, whose life has also been dictated by the addiction, no longer needs to face its consequences every day. She can relax, or can she? What if he doesn't last out? How long before he drinks, gambles, has an affair, spends all his wages in one go again?

If her partner has become abstinent he may be the focus of

praise, support and encouragement. The client, who may have at least received compassion for her plight, is now deprived of positive attention.

Moreover, problems do not disappear overnight once an addict stops the addiction. Financial problems may remain for a long time after. Family rifts may be slow to heal. And the addicts themselves will most likely be prone to overwhelming feelings, possibly depression or anger, that have been suppressed for so long through the addiction. Now as much as ever your client may need counselling and support. Allow her to express her anger safely. Encourage her to look at the change of roles brought about by her partner's abstinence. Talk with her about the possibility of relapse and her fears of it. Above all, if she has been going to a support group, encourage her not to leave at this point, but to continue taking support for herself through this difficult transition. She still has her own life to lead.

DISCUSSION ISSUES

1   Have you ever tried to fix someone who had a problem, addiction or otherwise. What happened? How did you feel?
2   Have you ever put yourself in the role of victim? What was the pay-off? And the consequences?
3   Have you counselled a bereaved person? What are the similarities and differences to counselling a client who is letting go of fixing an addicted partner?
4   How would you counsel a client if her partner did relapse?

4

Co-dependency as the Consequence of Childhood Abuse

So far I have looked at two manifestations of co-dependency in the adult. First, at how the co-dependent person may be using an addiction to cover up their painful feelings. Secondly, at how a co-dependent person is often the partner of an addict. In either case, co-dependents are, with varying degrees of success, managing to keep the focus off themselves. Why? If we look at the roots of co-dependency it becomes clear that painful childhood experiences of growing up in what I call a dysfunctional family are a universal factor. Family could mean a single-parent family, an adoptive family or perhaps social workers in a care setting, as well as the more traditional family. The experience of childhood abuse is one which most people would rather not face and so a distraction is sought. Equally, the experience results in a 'loss of self' which makes it easier for the co-dependent adult to focus on others whilst remaining unaware of their own feelings and needs.

Just as I asked you to open your mind to a wider definition of addiction, so I will ask you to consider a wider definition of child abuse.

TYPES OF ABUSE

Physical abuse

This is perhaps the form which first comes to mind when we mention child abuse, and one which often hits the headlines. A child's body is precious, and if it is attacked or beaten, the child's body is not safe. Everyone has the right to grow up feeling physically safe. An adult who has been physically abused may continue to abuse their body themselves through self-mutilation or substance abuse. She may choose a partner who physically abuses her, believing at some level that this is all she can expect. She may be unable to accept pleasurable physical experiences such as caresses, or she may dislike her body and keep it covered and hidden.

Less obvious physical abuse can include witnessing someone else being physically abused. A child may have watched his older brother being beaten, or his mother being hit. He may be filled with pain, fear, anger and guilt (that it was not him instead).

Equally, not being cared for physically is abusive. A child depends on an adult to keep him warm, clean, fed and safe, and then to teach him how to look after these needs himself. Not having your physical needs met is another form of physical abuse.

Sexual abuse

There was a time when sexual abuse was not acknowledged. Thankfully this has changed. A child is not ready physically or emotionally for sexual contact beyond their own natural curiosity and awareness. A child is not mature enough to give consent. If a child is sexually abused she is likely to experience damaging long-term effects. Many women who were sexually abused turn to drugs or become prostitutes, believing their bodies to be worthless. Both sexes may become sex addicts, acting out their rage by treating partners as sexual conquests. They may be unable to experience sexual intimacy. Men who have been sexually abused may feel even less able to share their 'secret' than women. This taboo is only slowly being broken down as men begin to speak out.

In the same way, whilst it has now been acknowledged that fathers sexually abuse daughters, the extent that mothers sexually abuse sons is only just coming to light.

There are many forms of less overt sexual abuse. Whilst it can and does mean rape of a child it also includes any sexualised touching of a child. When a child reaches puberty she needs privacy. Intruding on the child dressing or bathing without permission can be abusive, as can an adult displaying their body to the child. It is always the adult's responsibility to avoid sexually abusing a child. If a child is sexually provocative, or if a child enjoys the sexual contact, this does not mean the child is 'asking for it'. Many adults feel great shame and guilt if this was their experience as a child and need reassurance that they were not responsible for being abused.

Another form of sexual abuse occurs when a child is placed in the position of 'substitute spouse'; let's say a boy is required to act as husband to his mother. This may be because the father is physically absent, through death, separation or divorce. Or it may be that he is emotionally absent, possibly through an addiction such as work or alcohol. The mother turns to the boy to meet all the needs which should properly be met by her husband, an adult. The boy will feel powerful in being so important to his mother but may also fear his father's jealousy, knowing he has somehow replaced him, and inevitably feels burdened by the inappropriate intimacy and responsibility of his position. As a man he may choose needy dependent women as partners but then feel 'smothered' by them and abruptly end relationships. His fantasies may focus on unavailable women.

Emotional abuse

This is a wide category but I will try to indicate common forms of emotional abuse which can be damaging, all the more so because they are not always seen as child abuse in its strictest sense.

The family with a 'no-talk' rule cannot nurture a child. This family may look wonderful on the outside, but no one is allowed to name any of the problems. The child may sense tension and unhappiness, but no one talks about it. As an adult the child feels ashamed if he has problems, let alone if he tries to talk about them. He may experience physical discomforts or illness instead.

Another example of emotional abuse is in a family with inconsistent rules, for example the child is rebuked for being angry or loud, but one parent is seemingly allowed to rage and scream whenever it suits them.

Children may be subjected to verbal abuse. This could be screaming, criticism, taunting, shaming. It could be listening to one parent criticise the other parent, or a brother or sister. A child may not be allowed to express certain feelings, particularly anger or sadness. They may be told off if they cry. The disapproval may be directly communicated, or indirectly, for example a child may sense that her mother cannot cope emotionally if she expresses sadness to her. The child will seek parental approval above all, and will soon learn not to express those forbidden feelings. If this continues she may lose the sense of having those feelings. This causes problems which continue into adulthood. Suppressed anger can become rage, suppressed sadness can become despair, suppressed fear can become phobia.

Abandonment and engulfment

These are both forms of emotional abuse. Children can be physically abandoned, by death, separation of parents, by being placed in boarding school or in care. They can also be emotionally abandoned, by a parent's addiction, illness or simply their unavailability, most probably caused by them not receiving love themselves as children.

The child grows up fearful of further abandonment, and often believing that in some way he is 'bad' or else the parent would have been there for him. He may choose partners who are unavailable, and repeat the history of trying to win them over by being indispensable or perfect or whatever they want him to be. However if he finds someone who is available he will be frightened by the prospect of closeness, not having experienced it, and may well sabotage the relationship himself or push that person to reject him by behaving objectionably.

Engulfment often happens when the child is drawn into being a substitute spouse, as I describe under 'Sexual abuse'. It can also occur in families where for example there has been a death. If one family member has died, people can respond by closing ranks and becoming highly protective of the remaining members. At other times this happens in a family where the parents have an inability to reach outside for their needs. The family becomes fused, and children are also expected to get all their needs met within the family.

Children who are engulfed often find it hard to grow up and separate from their parents, but can easily feel overwhelmed or smothered by close relationships in adulthood. Paradoxically they too have been emotionally abandoned, for their true

40

needs – to be looked after and loved as children rather than as 'adult children' if they were substitute spouses, or to be allowed to explore and be social if they grew up in a fused family, have been neglected.

Pia Mellody offers two further categories of abuse – intellectual and spiritual. She describes intellectual abuse happening when children's thoughts are not respected, which she says can still be done even if the child's thoughts are flawed through immaturity. It can also happen if children are not taught how to solve or face life's little and big problems. Spiritual abuse is divided into two categories; one is abuse by a religious representative, which she sees as particularly damaging because it can often prevent someone from experiencing any form of spiritual comfort in future. The other category she describes as occurring when a parent or caregiver will not accept their own fallibility and be accountable for it (Mellody 1989: 177–93).

I hope that by enlarging on the accepted definitions of child abuse you will have changed your image of an abused child. Many co-dependents will say that they had a 'happy childhood' and this is often accepted. Maybe your client was not beaten or hit, but has he been allowed to separate from the family? Maybe your client was not sexually assaulted but was she drawn into a husband–wife relationship with her father?

CHILD DEVELOPMENT

So how does growing up in a family which is not functioning healthily affect a child's development? The answer is 'in many ways' and throughout the stages below I can only hope to give some examples.

Infancy

This is the stage when trust develops. The infant is dependent on the mother for all its needs and does not have a sense of self separate from her. If she is not there, if she does not respond to his cries, if she does not mirror his looks and movements, if he senses she does not enjoy spending time with him, how can trust develop? If she has an addiction she may well not be there for him. If she is a co-dependent of an addict husband her energy will be for him at the baby's expense. Some co-dependents are aware that from birth they were not wanted or welcomed and as adults often struggle with whether they themselves want to live.

Early childhood

This is the stage when the child reaches out and explores and also begins to gain a sense of himself as separate from other selves, hence the need to rebel described as the 'terrible twos'. If the child is from a fused family he may be given little space to explore – already his mother feels threatened by her own need to be his sole source of satisfaction. The child learns it is not safe to explore as it upsets his mother. Or his father. He stays close because that is when he is rewarded. If the child is in a family where feelings of anger are not expressed the parents may be unable to tolerate his tantrums. He may be shamed for them, or he may learn not to have them.

Play age

At this stage children are developing initiative and are looking to their parents as role models and question-answerers as they begin to form a sense of who they are and what life is about. They are at their most vulnerable to sensing the family rules and the fixed roles they have been assigned to meet the needs of the family system. If the child is prescribed a fixed role he must begin to act accordingly – i.e., don't rock the family boat. It is not safe for him to do just what he needs to do at this age – to change, to experiment and to grow. It may be at this stage that a child becomes aware if one or both parents are looking to the child to meet needs that each other cannot meet. The child will strive to meet them and in doing so develops an unhealthy sense of inappropriate responsibility. As adults, co-dependents often feel responsible for everyone else's behaviour and feelings.

This is also the age when children are discovering sexuality. They are curious about sex differences, their own bodies, others' bodies and their identity as a boy or girl. If parents or carers are not at ease with their own sexuality children soon learn that this is a shameful area, an unmentionable subject.

The consequence of childhood abuse

School age

If the child develops healthily at this age he will attain a feeling of competence. He will acquire skills in socialising in the wider world and begin to understand the need for inter-dependency and co-operation. If he can fit in and learn in this wider world he will sense his own power rather than inferiority. A child's ability to fit in and co-operate in the school world will be much determined by what is going on at home. He may already have learned at play age not to ask questions and take initiative. His sense of self may already be diminishing as he takes on the fixed role ascribed to him in his family. He may therefore feel unsure how to communicate in the wider world and repeat a pattern of adapting to what he imagines others want him to be. School can be a place where children are quickly judged by how bright they are, how fast they are, how tidy they are. If a child has developed a healthy self-esteem from nurturing within the family he will cope better with these judgements. If not, he may depend excessively on achievement for his self-worth or become competitive at the expense of co-operation. If a child's physical needs are not provided for at home, he may be singled out, taunted or isolated at school, e.g. if he is not washed or clothed properly. If he is being physically or sexually abused he may have begun to shut down and be unable to concentrate at school. Similarly if he has a sense of trying to hold his parents' marriage together. At this age, as the outside world begins to exert its influence, harsh judgement is so much harder to deal with if the child has not already developed an inner core of sufficient sense of self, trust, self-esteem and confidence.

Adolescence

Nearly all adolescents experience identity confusion and this is a normal part of growing up and becoming a unique, inde-pendent individual. Whilst this search may continue into our adult lives, during adolescence there is specifically (1) a need to choose what we want to accept and reject of our childhood identifications and (2) a need to be recognised and accepted by society, to belong, which may necessitate rejection of other

43

parts of society. Hence a teenager's need to identify with a certain fashion, style of music, ideology.

Those who came from a dysfunctional family will have great trouble with (1) above as it is unlikely they will have a clear sense of childhood identifications to sift through. As for (2), this is where an adolescent who has been abused may well choose to act out his hurt and anger, or act out the burden he has been carrying for the family. He may identify himself by associating with drugs, drink, crime or other behaviour which causes society to reject him at the same time as earning him negative attention. It may also be the time when he takes his fixed family role and begins to seek a purpose for it in the outside world. If he has been the family rescuer he may become devoutly religious, if he is the family hero he may become obsessed with achieving at school or college. In adulthood he may choose a career that follows on from this fixed role, and thereby sanctions it, e.g. the family rescuer becomes a social worker, the family hero becomes a managing director.

If the adolescent comes from a fused family he may be unable to complete the crucial distancing from family necessary if he is to become independent and individual. Teenagers develop a natural but often painful self-consciousness, the sense that everyone is looking at them. A co-dependent teenager, who has learned to stifle his real self and present a false self, will experience the feeling of being looked at as particularly threatening, for he is trying to remain hidden. He may feel shame for being who he is. Again this is an age of experimentation, and of sexual experimentation without commitment. The adolescent who has become a surrogate spouse will either subjugate her natural desires to her father's needs, or may rebel by becoming promiscuous. If she does the latter she may well then become the family scapegoat, the family problem. Olga remembers her feelings of guilt when after a first date at 14, her father moodily enquired why she preferred to go out with a boy she hardly knew when he could have taken her out that night. Still wanting her father's approval she soon ended what was after all a frivolous first relationship.

CONSEQUENCES OF ABUSE

Loss of self

So what is happening to the child growing up in a dysfunctional family? The overriding factor is that they are not being allowed to be themselves, whether this is that they are not allowed to trust, to be angry, to explore, to make mistakes, to be separate or to be a child, to name but a few examples. Because the child's aim is always to be acceptable to their caregiver the child adapts a false self. The real self is experienced as unwanted and flawed and the child feels shame about it. The false self is also a defence against that shame.

In Figure 2, Robert Subby illustrates the development of the false self as the child develops.

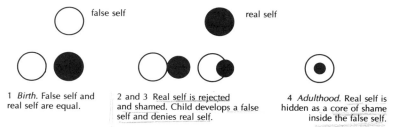

1 *Birth.* False self and real self are equal.

2 and 3 Real self is rejected and shamed. Child develops a false self and denies real self.

4 *Adulthood.* Real self is hidden as a core of shame inside the false self.

Figure 2   Development of the false self (adapted from Subby and Friel 1990)

The emerging co-dependent adult has not lost his real self. However, he is ashamed of it and keeps it well hidden. As I said at the beginning of this chapter, focus on another person or use of an addiction, or both, serve to keep it hidden. Health for a co-dependent involves recovering his real self and accepting his real self. As a counsellor, your first role may have been to encourage your co-dependent client to stop their life-threatening addiction, or to stop 'fixing' their partner. They may not have given up all their addictions and may not have totally given up on fixing their partner, but they may have given up enough to begin to focus on themself, and their real self may be emerging after years of being suppressed.

Your work will be most helpful if you concentrate on your client's adult issues as well as the childhood roots of his co-dependency. This chapter focuses on the latter.

I love and approve of myself.

Some clients may come to you fully aware of their childhood abuse, and of its effect. More likely, your client will be in denial about some or all of their childhood abuse. It is important to know how this denial operates.

Denial

Denial at the time the abuse takes place probably enables the victim to survive. This is true for children and adults. Brian Keenan's powerful description of his experience as a hostage is a case in point. In *An Evil Cradling* he describes variously being oblivious to the beatings, feeling energised by the violence, defending himself from fear and pain through hate, and laughing about it afterwards.

If children were to experience the reality of their abuse they might not have survived into adulthood, so defences are built up. Whilst these may be useful at the time, continuing to keep them up may not help the adult. For example, Khaled was beaten as a child. His defence was to shut down, as if surrounded by a wall. In adulthood this has become a wall of anger, which whilst it may still appear to protect him, keeps people away and prevents any close relationships. Paulette was sexually abused as a child, when she was treated as her father's surrogate wife. Because she does not recognise this as abusive she continues to pick men who step over her boundaries and are sexually aggressive. Ruth was verbally abused and criticised by her mother. Each time it happened Ruth would consciously dismiss it from her mind. She has always maintained that her mother was wonderfully loving, that their relationship was perfect. However, she was distressed by her compulsion to scold and humiliate her own daughter. Through counselling she is slowly beginning to remember the reality about her mother and see how she is repeating the pattern of abuse.

The above examples show that denial can take various forms. To make this clearer, I want to take one form of abuse and describe different ways a client might use denial.

Let's say that your client was sexually abused.

1   He may have automatically erased the experience from his

mind, or repressed it. If this has happened it may be hard for your client to recall. The memory may be lost forever.

2 He may have been aware of the abuse, but made a decision to forget it, i.e., the memory is suppressed. If so, the experience may be easier for your client to recall.

3 He may have been aware of the abuse, but removed himself from the experience, by mentally separating himself from his body. This is called dissociation.

4 He may have been aware of the abuse but minimised its effect. This minimisation could range from an overall belief that sexual abuse is ok, to acknowledging the harm of sexual abuse but maintaining that his experience of it wasn't that awful.

A client who has experienced child abuse and is still in some form of denial has invariably not had his pain and suffering validated. No one safe witnessed what was happening and stopped it, and no one was present for the child to confide in and then have his experience acknowledged as abuse. Dr Alice Miller was convinced that it was not so much the traumas we suffer in childhood which cause emotional crisis as the inability to express the trauma. As a counsellor one of your most crucial roles is to provide support and validation as your client moves out of denial and begins to feel their unresolved grief.

HEALING THE ABUSE

Unblocking denial

I believe there is a role for education when helping a client who is in denial about childhood abuse. By this I mean that a client needs exposure to a wider definition of childhood abuse in order for him to rank and define his own experiences. You could spend some sessions explaining the wider definition, but books or tapes on the subject would be another channel, and one which encourages your client to be active in his healing process rather than depending solely on you. I suggest that he covers one form of abuse at a time, reading the relevant material before using it to work on with you. I recommend that your client then does some writing work. Writing things down makes them more concrete and helps confront denial. Writing work about abuse can take two forms.

1 Take each category of abuse. For each category take each caregiver or significant adult (this could include parent, sister, brother, teacher, grandparent, friend of family, childminder). Detail how you now see that person was abusive to you.
2 Take each development stage as described earlier. Take each category of abuse. Detail how and by whom you were abused at each stage.

An example of (1) could be:

Physical abuse: mother

1 I think she didn't like changing my nappies and often used to leave me in wet ones.
2 She hit me when I was a toddler because I was clumsy and used to drop or spill things.
3 I hated watching her spank my younger brother. She used to spank him more than me, even if I was the naughty one.
4 She never cooked much for us. We had to come in from school and cook our own dinner.
5 My packed lunch at school was always cheap stuff. Other kids used to tease me about it.
6 When I came home later than I should once and brought my friend in with me she hit me in front of her.
7 I once saw her and auntie Carol have a fight on the street. I was terrified.

An example of (2) could be:

Infancy

1 My sister was jealous when I was born and I think I sensed she didn't want me there.
2 My mum and dad were so tied up with their marriage problems there was little time for me.
3 I think mum used to leave me on my own and go to the pub a lot.

The consequence of childhood abuse

Early childhood

1 I was told off if I cried, especially by dad. He said he'd give me something to really cry about if I didn't stop.
2 Mum left me with a childminder I didn't like. She shouted at me and the other toddlers there.
3 If I had a tantrum my sister would throw a bigger tantrum. I was told I'd started her off and that she was fine till I came along.
4 I'm not sure but I think I remember mum left home for a while. I don't know who looked after me then. It feels like no one did.

And so forth through each developmental stage. Let your client choose which form he uses – he may find it easier to focus on a person or on a time. Most people say that they don't remember their early years. Encourage your client to go with his guesses and instincts and begin to trust himself. Encourage your client to write down everything – even if he feels it to be trivial, selfish, ungrateful. Discourage him from rationalising or trying to understand it from the adult's perspective. Maybe his parents were poor and couldn't afford good packed lunches. Maybe big sister naturally felt jealous of a new arrival. Maybe mum couldn't help being alcoholic. Never mind. Your co-dependent client has spent enough time feeling sorry for others. Now it's time for him to grieve for himself and feel the pain he has pushed down for so long.

Don't think I am offering writing work as an easy solution or as *the* counselling tool. It is merely a starting point for what may be many emotional and difficult sessions with your client when all your skills as a counsellor will be called upon. Your client may still have to overcome problems of trust in you, idealising his parents, getting 'stuck', an inability to express his feelings and other obstacles to a satisfying outcome. What this kind of writing work does provide is a means to re-evaluate your client's perception of his childhood, a systematic memory prod and a method which makes avoidance of facts and feelings harder. When I did this work myself I realised that my unhappy childhood did not begin, as I had previously maintained, when I was 12. I had more grieving to do about my earlier years.

Groupwork

Writing work is even more effective if it is done with a group of clients. Each person writes their personal account of their childhood, but this is shared in the group. Often one client, on hearing another's story of abuse, will find that his memory is triggered. It is also helpful for others to learn that the abuse they thought was peculiar to their family existed in another's family, or that something they had felt pained about but dismissed as trivial is heard and validated as mattering by others in the group. At last their true feelings are accepted and the shame about them diminishes. It is particularly important if you are leading a group of this kind to make sure that each person has time to speak, possibly by setting a structure which allows a certain time for each participant. You may find it hard to restrict someone who is in full flow recounting a painful memory, but provided this is made clear beforehand the client will not experience this as uncaring. He may even find it provides safety and containment. Clients often feel that once they have begun to unleash childhood memories the flow is unstoppable. This can be overwhelming for the client and the rest of the group.

Body and feeling work

Memories do not always surface directly. Whilst a person may have forgotten or minimised their childhood abuse the memory is often held in the body or the emotions. As children many co-dependents escaped the pain in their bodies and their feelings by living in their head, whether by means of fantasy, reading books or watching television, or as they grew older by intellectualising, talking when they were scared, rationalising when they were angry. The pain stayed in their body and their emotions. The problem with counselling is that it can be head-focused. We can help our clients understand through thinking and talking, but it is also important to focus on our clients' body sensations and feelings where the past abuse may be trapped. Body language often gives us clues to a person's experience. The client who walks with a hollowed-in chest may still be holding in the physical abuse he received as a child. The client who speaks quietly and in a high pitch may still be holding in the emasculation he experienced through emotional sexual abuse. The client with stomach-ache may be holding in her anger against the father who raped her. Whilst body work should be done with an experienced body-work therapist, a good co-dependency counsellor can increase her client's body awareness by encouraging physical expression or bodily movement.

If a client is just describing a past event to you he may be staying in his head rather than recalling and refeeling the deep sensations which accompanied the event. True healing comes through re-experiencing the event rather than recounting it, and being allowed to stay with the feelings rather than suppressing them. Two-chair work (when a client talks to a significant person symbolised by an empty chair) combined with body awareness can facilitate this deep re-experiencing. To illustrate my point: Pushpa is talking as if to her mother, telling her how as a child she was always criticised whatever she did and that it made her feel like 'giving up'. Pushpa is crying but I notice her shoulders are tight and that the crying is subdued and impotent. I ask her to focus on her shoulders and she senses that they feel stuck. With encouragement she loosens and releases them and almost immediately her crying becomes strong and loud as she allows the despair to surface and be discharged.

We can also concentrate our clients on expressing their feelings as much as their thoughts. Very often, this involves slowing a client down when they are racing away with talk. It may mean a simple question: 'How do you feel as you tell me that?' or an encouragement to stay with the feeling, to allow the tears, to clench a fist as anger surfaces, to flop into the chair as feelings of hopelessness emerge.

You may also encourage your client to combine counselling with other physical activity. This could be dance, swimming, rugby, massage, Alexander technique, it doesn't matter what your client chooses, as long as it gets them 'out of their head'.

Inner child and reparenting work

Let's assume you have worked for some time with your client on their childhood abuse. Some relief is felt by your client as he grieves for what was missing or lost, and as his feelings are validated by you. This abused child is still carried within him, and often resurfaces when it is least useful for your adult client, e.g. he is still looking to girlfriends to parent him, to bosses to praise him, to friends to fill up his loneliness. Whilst all these people may do these things some of the time, expecting them to do them all of the time makes for unhappy, unhealthy relationships. Inner child and reparenting work is a powerful means of reclaiming that hurt child and starting to provide for the child what the family could not. In this work, you are asking your client to separate out their nurturing and responsible adult part from the hurt child inside and for that adult to reparent the child.

This work can be done individually or in groups. The client is guided through each developmental stage already described. Each stage should consist of an exploration, a guided visualisation and a follow-through. I use visualisations adapted from Bradshaw's *Homecoming*.

Exploration

Encourage your client to talk about as much as they know of that stage of their development. He can bring anything relevant along to the session, such as photos, toys, school books. He can include what he now knows as an adult, e.g. he now knows his father was not away on business but was in prison, and he can include guesses and intuition. Help your client by asking questions, explaining what a child needs at that stage.

Visualisation

Visualisations are a means of stimulating the imagination, mentally and emotionally, to create a picture of something new. This is sometimes called a guided fantasy. The counsellor acts as the guide, reading a passage aloud to the client, who is encouraged to 'live out' the fantasy in their mind. In the context of reparenting, the client is helped to build an image of a nurturing parent who is present at each stage of childhood. They visualise themselves as both the parent and the child. This serves two purposes: (1) it can act as a catharsis, enabling the client to grieve for what they did not have in their real childhood; (2) it can provide a healing experience as the client's 'inner child' senses how good it feels to be nurtured and given permission to be true to themselves.

Whilst this can be seen as a form of regression work, it is controlled rather than spontaneous. The client can stop the visualisation at any time if the images or feelings become overwhelming.

Follow-through

Again, this work is not an end in itself and should not be used as such. Do not have a rigid programme of working through the stages week by week. Allow your client to express related feelings. Sometimes you may question the relevance, but this usually becomes clear. For example, Karen worked on the infancy stage and felt unmoved and unable to reclaim that part of herself. We then spent many sessions talking about trust and her lack of trust in herself (you remember that the infancy stage is all about trust). We also explored how her inability to express anger sapped her energy. At a further session she read to me a letter (not intended for posting) she had written to her parents, expressing anger at them and telling them that her baby self was now with her and not them. Increasing trust in herself and release of anger had allowed her to move forward.

Working with a client on their childhood abuse takes time and is a painful process. However, for a co-dependent client, it is essential that he does this work if he is to heal the hurt child inside him. For it is the hurt child who has adapted the false self we recognise as an adult co-dependent. How does the adult survive meanwhile? Must he wait until all his childhood trauma is resolved before he can function more happily? My next chapter will look at ways to draw out and strengthen the healthy adult in a co-dependent client.

DISCUSSION ISSUES

1 Can you think of something which happened in your childhood, or to someone you know, which you might now describe as abusive, in its wider sense?

2 What stops children being angry with their parents? What stops them as adults?

3   What would you do if you suspected your client had been sexually abused and they denied it?

4   Why might a client be unwilling to reclaim and own their inner child?

5

Co-dependency as Loss of Self

In the previous chapter I examined how a co-dependent's loss of self comes about. Not having a sense of who you are can lead to severe difficulties in adult life. Grieving the childhood abuse at its root can enable your client to heal some of the shame she feels about her true self as she sees that it was not 'all her fault'. She can also begin to take care of the hurt child inside her.

However, on a day-to-day basis she needs to survive as an adult. Whilst she is healing the past she may still be using unhelpful patterns from the past to deal with the present. Whilst she may understand where her problems began she may find that this does not necessarily enable change.

When a co-dependent begins to discard her false self and expose her real self, the real self has been stuck in a state of stagnation for many years. It has not been allowed to grow and mature. New skills and new attitudes need to be learned and experimented with as you draw out the healthy adult in your client. Boundaries are invariably a problem for co-dependents.

BOUNDARIES

This is a word often used in counselling, but what does it mean?

A boundary is where I stop and the environment begins. It defines the difference between what is me and what is not me. A boundary is where contact ends and begins.

If there is not a boundary contact may overwhelm me. If the boundary is too powerful I may not achieve contact.

For example if I wear a flimsy shirt whilst pruning the roses my body may be scratched. However if I wear a suit of armour, besides looking very odd, my movements will be restricted and pruning will be difficult. I need appropriate clothing (boundary) to make appropriate contact with the rose bush (environment).

I hope this shows that we need boundaries both to keep us safe and to allow us to make contact.

A co-dependent often has problems with boundaries because her own have not been respected when she was growing up.

How boundaries can be damaged

Physical boundaries

If a child was physically or sexually abused her boundaries were certainly stepped over, if not trampled down. As an adult she may have little sense of her physical boundaries. She often lets them be invaded, or if she tries to put up a boundary she feels ashamed. Alternatively, she may have reacted to this invasion by building a symbolic suit of armour which no one can get through.

For example: as an adult Siobhan has difficulty saying 'no' to sexual contact she does not enjoy. She has told you that as she begins to heal from the original abuse she is learning to say 'no'. However, earlier in the week she had told her partner not to touch her breasts in a certain way. He had become angry and withdrawn sexually. She felt 'terrible'.

'Terrible' meant that she felt she had caused her partner's anger. She believed she had hurt him and made him feel inadequate. She also experienced his sexual withdrawal as abandonment, which fostered her underlying belief: 'I have no right to set my sexual boundary and if I do people will punish me and/or leave me. A man's sexual needs come first.'

Emotional and mental boundaries

If a child was emotionally or intellectually abused again his boundaries were not respected. As an adult he may have little sense of these boundaries or of his right to set them.

For example: Mark was continually told by his father that

he was stupid, wrong, hopeless. As an adult he is afraid to express his opinion in case he is seen as stupid and rejected by others. If someone puts forward a strong opinion Mark often agrees with it, only to agree with the opposite opinion voiced by another later that same day. Sometimes he doesn't even know what his own views are. He is now going out with someone who respects him but already he can sense that he is moulding himself to suit his new partner and taking on her radical political stance which he is actually unsure about.

In both these cases contact with others can feel abusive because the client's boundary is too thin, or non-existent. It is equally possible for someone to build up a boundary which is too thick and impenetrable. In this case contact, even pleasurable contact, is prevented.

Furthermore it is likely that someone whose own boundaries are damaged will be unaware of another person's need for boundaries. The client with no sexual boundary may have such a need for physical comfort that she in her turn hugs friends who do not like hugs, or strokes her partner's face when they are in company despite him telling her it embarrasses him. The client with a damaged boundary may try to control other people's feelings and behaviour. He may be unable to respect his new girlfriend's need to sometimes feel sad and constantly offer her solutions rather than allow her to stay with her feelings.

So how can the counsellor help a client develop good boundaries – ones which are firm but flexible?

Identification

First it is important to help your client identify which boundary was breached. She then needs to explore that experience and determine the message she is carrying as a result.

Here are some guidelines for questions you might use to facilitate this exploration.

1 Which boundary – physical, emotional, mental? Was more than one of them breached?
2 Who breached it? May be more than one person. How did they breach it? Give as much detail and as many examples as you can remember.

3 What was the message (begin with 'I have no right to . . .')? For example, 'I have no right to say no to violence' (physical); 'I have no right to think my own thoughts' (mental).
This is for people who have damaged, or no boundaries. For those who have set up impenetrable boundaries they may have transferred this message into 'No one can ever . . .'. For example: 'No one can ever touch me sexually' (physical); 'No one can ever criticise me' (mental); 'No one can ever make me cry' (emotional).

For those who have no boundary, or a damaged one, it is time to develop one. First explore with your client how this impaired boundary leaves them vulnerable as an adult. You may ask them to do this as a homework exercise, noting down at the end of the day how they got hurt through their lack of boundaries. Tracy was amazed when she reported back to me how many times in one day she allowed other people's comments about her new job to make her begin to think she had made the wrong decision. Ravi realised that whilst he could stand up to criticism from men, he allowed women to put him down because of his belief that he had no right to feel angry with women.

Visualisations

Visualising a boundary can help a client begin to protect herself.
Below is the visualisation I use for a client wanting to develop a sexual boundary. It can be adapted to any boundary and to include any particular message your client is carrying. When reading it out, allow fifteen-second pauses where indicated by ellipses.

Make yourself comfortable . . . Close your eyes and let your hands rest palm upwards . . . Feel where your body is in contact with the chair . . . Let your bottom and your back sink deeper into the chair and feel it hold you . . . Become aware of any part of you that is tense and consciously relax that part . . . Become aware of any worries or distractions . . . Let them surface . . . and as you breathe out let them go . . . Focus on your breathing . . . Feel the air as you breathe it in ... and as you breathe it out ... Imagine you are walking down a long flight of stairs ... Walk down each one slowly as I count down from ten ... 10, 9, 8, 7, 6, 5, 4, 3, 2, 1 ... When you reach the bottom of the stairs walk down a long corridor ... At the end of the corridor is a door. Open it and walk into a room ... Feel the warmth of the room as you walk in ... Look around and notice your surroundings ... In the room there is a choice of protectors which will help you keep your sexual boundary firm and flexible. You will control when, how and with whom you are sexual ... Choose your protector ... It might be a jacket, a second skin, a coat that reaches to the ground, a glass dome, a space suit ...

Go over to it and touch it ... What does it look like? ... What does it feel like? ... How does it protect you? ... Does it have magical qualities? ...

Now put it on or get inside it. Claim it as yours ... Walk around the room. Look at the room from inside your protector ... How do you feel? ...

Tell youself that now you have found and claimed your protector you can have a sexual boundary ... Tell yourself: [now make an affirmation which contradicts the received negative message – e.g. 'I have a right to decide when and how and with whom I will be sexual'] ...

Tell yourself that no one can take your protector away from you ... Walk back up the corridor, looking at your surroundings, this time from inside your protector ...

Walk up the stairs one at a time as I count up from one to ten ... 1, 2, 3, 4, 5, 6, 7, 8, 9, 10 ... Now become aware of this room ... Become aware of the sounds around you ... Feel your body in the chair ... Wriggle your toes ... and your fingers ... Touch your face ... When you are ready open your eyes and be fully present in the room again.

Let your client talk about what feelings and thoughts came up for her. Was she able to visualise her protector? Did she claim it and step into it? Or did she find herself unable to do so? If the latter, spend some time talking about her resistance, her fears, her pay-offs for not having a boundary.

If your client has positively taken on her protector, as well as talking about this you might ask her to draw it. After a few minutes ask her to present her protector to you describing every aspect in the first person as if *she* were the protector – e.g. 'I'm a long invisible magic coat. I protect her from any unwanted touches.'

Or you might ask your client to imagine her protector is on a chair in front of her and encourage a dialogue between client and protector, with your client moving back and forth between the chairs and always speaking in the first person.

In subsequent sessions continue to use the image and ask your client to visualise her protector around her whenever she is in a situation where her sexual boundary is needed. At that time she may also verbalise, silently or out loud if possible, the affirmation which replaces her old message.

Building a boundary that has not existed, or is weak, is slow work. Your client may well continue to let the boundary slip in the early days. The important thing is that she does not beat herself up about this, but simply notices it, reminds herself why she has problems with that boundary and resolves to set it more firmly the next time. She may wish to repeat the visualisation with you in order to strengthen or change her image.

How can we work with someone who has built up an inflexible boundary in response to the original transgression? The first exercise of identification is equally relevant. Once this has been explored, their homework might be to note down how they prevented contact through their inflexible boundary.

Sharlene never allows criticism. Her colleague tells her she thinks she has begun to make more typing errors recently and wonders if everything is ok at work. Sharlene immediately turns on her and tells her *her* typing is not so hot either. The colleague walks away hurt, her underlying concern unheard. She vows not to say anything more.

Shaun is frightened of closeness. He is invited on a camping trip with a group of friends. He spends several weeks worrying about whether he will be funny enough, interesting enough, fit enough and eventually turns down the offer. The friends remark to themselves that Shaun never wants to come away with them and decide he thinks he is too good for them. They don't invite him again.

This sort of boundary is usually made up of anger or fear – both of which can keep other people away. Explore with your client what it would be like to bend this boundary a little. What are her fears and fantasies of what would happen if she did so? You might ask your client to draw her boundary, or to draw herself as she might see herself without her boundary. Ask your client to describe the boundary she has drawn, speaking in the first person as the boundary. This helps the client to gain insight into the function of her boundary and her fears of being without it rather than rationalising and explaining. People with rigid boundaries often envisage an all-or-nothing situation, for example, either I keep my boundary as it is, or I throw it away and become completely defenceless. If your client has drawn her boundary as it is she could experiment with images of a new boundary which is protective but flexible.

Again self-awareness rather than judgement will help your client to change. Encourage her to simply notice when she uses the old boundary, and to notice and take credit when she succeeds in using the new one.

Mental and emotional boundary repair

Many co-dependents whose mental and/or emotional boundaries are damaged have difficulty in making decisions. They may be unclear what they think and what their views are (a natural consequence of having little sense of self) or they may be unable to trust their ability to make decisions and be immobilised by the fear of 'getting it wrong'.

Equally they have difficulty in knowing what they feel or, if they know, they fear stating what they feel (or think). As a result they often unnecessarily justify their thoughts and feelings with long explanations. This can undermine the strength of a simple statement and the listener may well pay less attention. A vicious circle, for the co-dependent will explain their listener's disinterest as a sign that their feelings or thoughts are wrong, or worthless.

Another reason for a co-dependent not knowing what he feels may be the long-term effects of an emotional conversion process. Let me explain. Growing up in a dysfunctional family, Stephen was not allowed to express fear or sadness. In his family, anger was the acceptable emotion. He learned that if he felt hurt or frightened it was fine to shout and roar. Eventually anger became the only emotion he experienced. As an adult his needs are often unmet because he cannot express the full range of emotions. In the same way Siobhan was not allowed to express anger in her family. When, as an adult, something triggers her anger, she often recognises it only after the event and is left with feelings of resentment or depression (anger turned in on herself).

If you have a client with these problems you may like to start your session with a simple exercise to encourage her to know and trust her own thoughts and feelings.

1 Encourage your client to relax with her eyes closed.
2 Ask her to focus inwards on her inner, true self and to begin to listen to this voice.
3 Encourage her to search for one feeling she has at this moment; if possible the feeling should be simplified to one of the four basic emotions – fear, anger, sadness, happiness.
4 Encourage her to search for one thing she has a view about at the moment, whether on the state of the world, or something personal.
5 Ask her, when she is ready, to open her eyes, look at you, and tell you: 'One feeling I have right now is . . . (name emotion) . . . and one thing I think right now is that . . .' (express view).
6 Tell your client that you just want the statements without any back-up or explanation.
7 Don't omit to explain the purpose of the exercise as outlined above, or to reassure her that she may feel uncomfortable about not justifying her stat ›ments and that this is a natural reaction at first.
8 Stop your client if she tries to explain at a later stage in the session. Tell her you accept both the statements as they stand. You may however want to explore her discomfort at not explaining. If you persist with this exercise she may well find it easier and be able to extend the exercise more and more to outside situations.

DECISION-MAKING

If your client is presented with a big or small decision she finds difficult encourage her to make the decision herself. Co-dependents often run from one person or one book to another seeking the solution outside of themselves. It is far better for your client to listen to various advice and then go away with all the information and different viewpoints and tune into her own wisdom to make her own decision. Her true self needs exercising if it is to develop, and part of developing and growing is to make mistakes. A co-dependent does not allow mistakes and needs to learn how to.

One corrective method for decision-making is for your client to move away from the fear of making the wrong decision. This can be done by reframing the dilemma into a more positive choice, e.g. whichever decision I take, what are the gains?

If she can see that there are gains to be made through either decision and that the choice is between different gains, the decision can feel less onerous. Co-dependents also need reassurance that most decisions are not irreversible; if your client transfers and does not like her new job she will not have to stay there forever.

SELF-ESTEEM

Co-dependents have low self-esteem and are slow to hear praise, whilst they will focus to the point of despair on one small criticism or one small mistake.

Cognitive and rational-emotive therapy are useful in countering low self-esteem and accompanying depression. Albert Ellis, who developed rational-emotive therapy, pointed out that feelings are not facts and that it is not so much things which cause us to feel or behave as we do, but how we view those things. Clients are encouraged towards rational beliefs, i.e., those which help us achieve our basic goals and purposes, rather than irrational beliefs, which prevent this. Irrational beliefs are challenged and questioned until the client acknowledges that there is no conclusive evidence which supports the belief. The client is then helped to formulate a rational belief instead. Please refer to the 'Further reading' list if you are interested in this therapy. For now, let me give you an example of it in practice when working with low self-esteem.

Del believes that she is useless and feels depressed because a friend has told her she wishes to end their friendship. The problem is not so much what her friend has told her, but how

Del has interpreted what her friend said, according to her irrational beliefs. These include:

1 If someone stops liking me I must have done something wrong.
2 If I do something wrong it means I am useless.
3 Everyone must always like me.
4 How valuable I am is measured by how many friends I have.
5 Because one friend has stopped liking me everyone else will do so too.

As a counsellor my role was to challenge all of Del's irrational beliefs which follow on from her friend's action and lead to her lowered self-esteem. She can learn to replace her irrational beliefs with more rational ones.

1 If someone stops liking me I might have done something wrong but there could be many other reasons.
2 If I do something wrong it doesn't make me a useless person.
3 It would be nice if everyone always liked me but it's unlikely, and not absolutely necessary.
4 My value as a person does not depend on the number of friends I have.
5 There is no reason for other people to stop liking me just because this friend has. I haven't changed to any extent over the past week.

Del needs to exercise these new beliefs in order for them to strengthen and wipe out the old beliefs. This takes time and effort on her part.

Implications of client's low self-esteem for the counsellor

Counselling tends to focus on a client's problems, but it is important that we never forget that there is a healthy core to everyone, if we can only tap into it. Make time in counselling to focus your client on their accomplishments and strengths, on what they find pleasurable and satisfying in life. I have sometimes found it appropriate to negotiate setting up one session as a 'positives' session. There is usually resistance to such a task and the client is often angry. A session, or half a session, or even ten minutes of a session when your client is asked to focus on what she is good at, what she likes about herself, what she has accomplished so far in life, in the past week, in counselling, is a useful exercise. As well as encouraging your client to derive her own self-esteem, the accompanying feelings of discomfort about positives are useful to explore.

Co-dependent clients with low self-esteem are prone to setting up their counsellors as gurus, or experts. This is unhelpful for both of you. Appropriate self-disclosure is a good way to bring you back down to earth and prevent your client suffering from a crick in the neck. Counsellors are not there to advise clients; this is even more important than usual when working with co-dependents who may manipulate you into this role so that they can stay one-down. Allow your client to find her own answers and her own interpretations.

A client-centred counselling model as defined by Carl Rogers can be useful for working with co-dependent clients, as it emphasises three core conditions – congruence, or genuineness, empathy and unconditional positive regard. If you are congruent as a counsellor you can avoid the guru role. Your client will learn from your genuine responses that you are an equal human being with your own feelings and the capacity to make, and acknowledge, mistakes. Mutual trust develops through mutual respect, rather than being expected automatically. Also empathy – in order to feel the client's world as she feels it. Co-dependents often feel alienated and misunderstood but also doubt that they are *worth* understanding. Try to develop unconditional positive regard – this is something co-dependents did not receive whilst growing up. Being accepted 'just as they are' is a healing experience and allows them to begin to feel unconditional self-acceptance.

USE OF AFFIRMATIONS

Counsellors working with co-dependents recommend the use of affirmations as a means of replacing negative messages and self-images and building up positive thoughts about oneself. The negative messages could be seen as the irrational beliefs I discussed earlier. Affirmations serve two purposes: (1) to build up positive statements and self-image; (2) to 'flush out' all the negative shaming messages, some of which may be buried in the unconscious.

Whilst there are plenty of books and tapes suggesting positive affirmation, encourage your client to choose her own, as they will be different for each person. She may wish to do this by making a list of all the 'bad' things she thinks about herself and then reframing them into positive statements, for example:

I am ugly. – I am beautiful in every way.
I am lazy. – I put every effort into what I do.
I am selfish. – I have a right to take care of my needs.

Research suggests that in order to be effective each affirmation is best written and spoken aloud fifteen to twenty times daily for a minimum of three weeks.

The effect of writing out such affirmations is to bring out the negative counter-messages in their full force. Encourage your client to write alongside the affirmation each negative thought which accompanies it, for example:

I am clever and creative. – I am stupid.
I am clever and creative. – Who do you think you are!
I am clever and creative. – I am boring and stupid.

From past experience I would recommend that you ensure your client has a good support system to draw on between sessions if she is doing this as homework, as its effect can be powerful and overwhelming. You can also help by preparing her beforehand to expect the negative messages to surface. It's important that she does not stop the exercise before it is completed. If she does complete it she will find the negative messages wearing thin and the right column may now contain, as in a recent client's case, 'Yes I am!' I believe affirmation work is only fully effective if the counter-messages are explored and worked through. Often the counter-messages are found to be introjected parental messages, i.e., parental rules or criticisms your client has swallowed whole. By externalising them your client then has more choice about whether she wants to continue to accept them or if they need spitting out.

In addition to affirmations work you might encourage your client to write an abundance diary. This has a similar purpose – to counteract a co-dependent's frequent sense that 'there is never enough', and their tendency to 'awfulise'. An abundance diary is as simple as it sounds – each day your client's diary entry denotes what was positive for them. Writing it can become a pleasurable experience, as can rereading it at a later date, particularly when it covers a time the client remembers as unhappy or difficult. This kind of work is particularly helpful in encouraging your client to find balance.

FROM VICTIM TO RESPONSIBILITY

I have mentioned the co-dependent client playing the victim role in earlier chapters. This can cause problems in adult life and in the counselling session itself.

Encourage your client to take responsibility for herself and her life and in your sessions together. Whilst she may not be responsible for everything that happens to her she can be responsible for how she responds and how she treats others in this world. Challenge your client when she blames and becomes the angry victim, or when she plays 'poor me' and becomes the helpless victim. Encourage her to think in terms of 'can, will, choose to' rather than 'should, must and have to'.

You may wish to use and teach the Karpman Drama

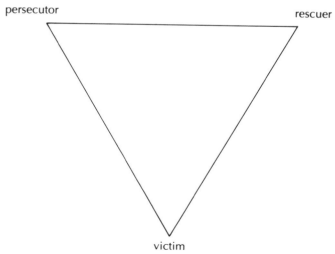

Figure 3   The Karpman Drama Triangle

Triangle to assist self-awareness about responsibility. This was developed in the late 1960s by Stephen Karpman to untangle the victim mentality and the games we get caught up in when we take on certain roles.

When playing this game the client puts responsibility for their feelings into others' hands. It happens frequently in relationships where one or both partners are co-dependent. Both usually begin by playing victim or rescuer – no one likes to be seen as a persecutor. However, if the rescuer's attempts to rescue are rejected by the victim, the rescuer will easily slide into persecutor. Equally if the victim moves from helpless victim to angry victim they can then become persecutor as they release blame and rage in an attempt to manipulate the other person back into rescuer. A vicious triangle!

Rescuers need to feel needed and need to control others in order to avoid their own feelings. This is particularly common amongst co-dependents of addicts. Victims need to avoid taking responsibility for how they feel and what they do. This is common amongst co-dependents who felt overly responsible as children, or who were scapegoats in their family. Persecutors need to find fault in others and win at all costs. This may stem from rage and powerlessness from childhood.

However anyone can move in and out of all three roles and all three roles are an avoidance of honest feelings.

GENDER AND CO-DEPENDENCY

Whilst both men and women can be co-dependents, the stereo-typed roles according to gender that our society prescribes for us sanctify many co-dependent behaviours. In working with co-dependency let's not forget the influence of sexual politics on our clients' personal lives, which can prevent realisation of their true selves as much as their individual history can.

Women

It's not ok to look how you look. You must be slim, blonde, sexy, hairless, pretty, small, short, not have spots, wear glasses or sweat.

It's not ok to be independent, successful, selfish, sexual, single, lesbian, black, without children, disabled, old.

Co-dependency as loss of self

It's good to look after, rescue, enable, caretake, sacrifice, keep a good home.

Don't be angry or loud or too clever.

Men

It's not ok to look how you look. You must be big, tall, handsome, athletic, hairy, broad-chested, have a big penis. You must not have spots, wear glasses or be bald.

It's not ok to be dependent, sexually shy, unambitious, gay, black, disabled.

It's good to be sexually aggressive, have affairs, be a workaholic, to hold your drink like a man, to win and achieve, drive a car.

Don't cry or be sad or frightened.

RACE AND CO-DEPENDENCY

In this country racism, both personal and institutional, is a fact of life for people from cultural or ethnic minorities. Many are attacked or shamed simply because of the colour of their skin.

Many are denied access to good housing, education and health resources, as the black community here is predominantly working-class. Those who succeed speak of the need to acquire a strong self-identity against all odds.

For co-dependent black clients, feeling bad about themselves inside can often be projected outside by borrowing racism's image of black being inferior, dangerous or bad. They may then identify negatively with their own race or culture or deny their separate racial identity (Kareem and Littlewood 1992: 142). The helplessness they may have felt as a child in an unnurturing family may be intensified when experiences of racism are felt as a lack of control over external events. If they were shamed by their family for who they were, growing up and reaching beyond the family in a racist society means being then shamed for their culture or race. Racism is much harder to fight if society confirms your feelings of already being 'less than'.

In addition, black and ethnic minority people are stereotyped in our society, e.g. Afro-Caribbeans as aggressive, 'sexy', Asians as passive, materialistic. None of this allows people to be accepted just as they are.

It is widely acknowledged nowadays that good self-esteem in black people has a direct correlation to a positive racial identity. Black co-dependent clients may therefore wish to work with a black counsellor, but if they work with a white counsellor, through choice or otherwise, it is the counsellor's responsibility to acknowledge and work with the issue of racial difference. A white counsellor can also encourage their client to identify with black groups and movements and to find positive role models from their own race.

DEPENDENCY AND INTIMACY

To survive as a healthy adult I need to know how to take care of myself. This means that I need to know what I need and what I want to make myself comfortable and happy. If I am healthy I can acknowledge these needs and wants without feeling ashamed of them. If I cannot meet them myself I need to be able to ask for help without shame and without an overwhelming fear of my request being rejected.

Co-dependents have problems in these areas. Your client may be unable to recognise her wants and needs or may confuse them. This is particularly common if as a child her wants and needs were ignored. She learned not to have any. As an adult, when she needs company she may think she wants a chocolate bar instead. She may spend a night out late and realise the next day that what she had needed was to stay in and go to bed early.

If as a child she was shamed for expressing needs and wants she may recognise them as an adult but be fearful of voicing them. She feels ashamed of them and thinks of herself as demanding, greedy or selfish. She may spend an afternoon listening to a friend in distress when she herself needed a listening ear that day.

If she asks for help and the other person is unable to meet her need she experiences it as a total rejection and feels either angry or ashamed, or both. She may never ask so that she never risks a negative response.

Equally she may overdepend on others and refuse to take care of herself. If her partner goes away for the weekend she feels lost and resentful instead of using the time to see friends, or follow interests her partner might not share. When her partner returns she feels unable to welcome her home and cries that she cannot live without her.

Identify with your client which area of dependency is particularly difficult for her.

Knowing her needs and wants. Ask her to make a mental (or, if practical, written) note of 'what do I need and what do I want' at least once a day. When she experiences a want ask her to check out if it *is* a want, or a cover-up for a need, e.g. 'I want some chocolate' may be covering up 'I need some affection'. Particularly relevant if she has an active addiction. It may be a genuine want and that is ok. If we can meet our wants it can make us happy.

Accepting her needs and wants. Ask your client to write a list of needs and wants she often experiences, and then to read them out to you. Which does she feel most ashamed of? Can she add any by starting with: 'If I didn't think you'd judge me for it I'd tell you that I need/want . . .'? Explore with your client the beliefs underlying her most shameful needs and wants. How would it be if they were met?

Asking for help and risking rejection. An exercise for your client is to decide one thing she will ask for help with and from whom before the next session. It should be a small thing but one that involves a little risk. Your client may wish to role-play it first with you. If she does not manage the task take time in the next session to look at how she avoided it. Look also at the consequences – did she do the thing herself, did the need or want go unmet?

Over-dependency. Ask your client to list all the things she doesn't do for herself because she wants others to do them for her. How many of them do not get done? How many things does she not do because she wants to do them with other people? Is there one she can make a commitment to doing on her own?

In my experience self-care improves as the client's self-esteem improves and as her sense of self emerges and is accepted by herself and others.

A person cannot enjoy intimacy in sexual relationships unless they have resolved their dependency problems, and are able to be interdependent with another. Co-dependents tend either to depend excessively on their partner, when their partner experiences them as stifling, or to be unable to depend on their partner, when their partner experiences them as invulnerable. Often two co-dependents will pair up – one overdependent, the other unable to depend and in this way they perpetuate each other's difficulty.

Intimacy also requires that a co-dependent works on the other issues in this chapter. Good flexible boundaries are needed for your client to feel safe enough to get close! Good self-esteem is needed if your client is to form a relationship with someone who offers respect. And in an intimate relationship each person must take responsibility for their feelings and be able to voice them honestly. The desire for a good, intimate relationship may be what drives your client to recover from co-dependency. Recovery from co-dependency means recovering one's real self and embracing it with self-acceptance. This is the most important relationship. Better relationships with others and a greater capacity for intimacy are welcome bonuses.

DISCUSSION ISSUES

1 Has someone ever breached your boundary? How did you feel and how did you react?

2 Can someone have a good sense of self and still have low self-esteem?

3 Are there groups in society you find hard to accept 'just as they are'?

4 Where do you draw the line in a person being responsible for not being a victim?

6

Co-dependency and You

I think of this as a 'last but not least' chapter. Good counsellors
take a long hard look at themselves to see if they too have
unresolved issues, and, more importantly, if these issues might
affect the way they work with clients. This is ongoing work
and usually forms an integral part of supervision and self-
assessment. I want to look briefly at how co-dependency in
counsellors can make us less than useful.

There is growing evidence that many co-dependents choose
a job in which they can become professional caretakers. This
job might be social work, nursing, counselling or any of the
other so-called caring professions where there is an opportunity to 'fix' someone else, to help others. Those who grew up
in families that did not meet their needs learned to deny their
needs by taking care of others' needs, and learned that this
was one way of regaining a sense of self-worth that they did
not have just by being. It made them feel important, it made
them feel needed, it gave them a chance to control in a 'helpful
way', it took away some of their own pain. They may have
begun to do so with family and friends. Then they found they
could make a career of it!

I've not saying that all counsellors are co-dependent, nor
that all co-dependents become counsellors. Moreover, if you
have recognised yourself in the preceding chapters, don't
despair, I am not suggesting you have chosen the wrong direc-
tion. A person who recognises their co-dependency and works
on it can be an excellent counsellor. If you do not consider
yourself co-dependent I suggest you nevertheless read this
section. As I suggested in the introduction, most people have
difficulty in some of these areas some of the time.

73

CARETAKING

If we are caretaking we are not being good counsellors. A good counsellor cares about her clients but she doesn't take care of them – she allows them to take care of themselves, whilst she takes care of herself. She knows that whilst she can be there for her clients she cannot solve their problems nor take away their pain. She is aware that making herself indispensable to her clients is not helpful to them. Rather, it can create an unhealthy dependency whereby the client's well-being depends largely on their counsellor being part of their life and where the counsellor's love, approval and affirmation replaces the client's need for self-esteem.

If we know we are caretakers or that this forms part of our role as counsellors, there is no need for shame. We can doubtless trace our need to caretake and understand the purpose it once served. Then we can begin to redress it.

1 What needs of your own are you avoiding?
2 How else can you develop a sense of your own worth?
3 What are the possible harmful effects on your individual clients?

PEOPLE-PLEASING

If we are stuck with a need to people-please we cannot fulfil our role as counsellors. A good counsellor does not need his clients' approval in order to feel good about himself. He knows that there are times he needs to confront his clients and say difficult things they may not want to hear. He also recognises that his people-pleasing comes from a wish to avoid conflict and deflect anger, but that conflict and anger are a normal part of any relationship, including a counsellor–client relationship.

1 Are there things you are avoiding saying to a client?
2 Are you deflecting a client's anger?
3 How easy is it for your clients to be angry with you?

KARPMAN TRIANGLE

If you are stuck in your work with a client, check out the Karpman Triangle. It may be appropriate to do this alone or in supervision, or it may feel right to use it openly with your client. Has you client dug himself in as a victim and are you trying to rescue him? Are you feeling angry (persecutor) with him because your efforts are failing? Are you feeling like the victim of your client's unreasonable behaviour? Are you needing to rescue a particular client (maybe because their pain triggers off your own) and thereby reinforcing their role as helpless victim?

SELF-CARE ISSUES

If we are not taking care of ourselves, or are not aware of our needs and wants we cannot be good counsellors. Counsellors need:

A comfortable and safe working environment

1 Do you have comfortable chairs you can relax in?
2 Is the room warm/cool enough?
3 Is the decor adequate? Is it pleasant?
4 Are you free from interruptions during a session?
5 Is there enough privacy for the client to scream or cry?

Support

1 Do you have good, frequent supervision?
2 Where do you get support in addition to, and in between supervision sessions?
3 Do you have a policy for dealing with emergencies such as violence?

Rest

1 How long an interval do you take between counselling sessions?
2 How much holiday do you take?
3 Do you take time off when sick?
4 What do you do to relax/escape/have fun?

SELF-ESTEEM

Good counsellors are continually building their self-esteem and don't look to their clients' approval to feel good about themselves. Equally they are able to model healthy imperfections, to know when it is appropriate to acknowledge a mistake to a client and to be able to do so without plummeting into the abyss! My self-esteem took a knock when I worked with a client who was a counsellor herself. Even before she arrived for her first session I had decided she probably knew more than me and that I would feel inadequate. As a result I allowed her to take control of the first session and was hesitant in my communication. Good supervision enabled me to see how frightened she was and how she needed me to reassert my authority and confidence if she was to feel safe. Although I knew I had made a bit of a mess of that session, my own work on my self-esteem allowed me to laugh about it and regain my confidence and skills the next week. It's certainly true that if we position ourselves as 'less than', our creativity is paralysed and our natural curiosity becomes inhibited as we focus on our performance anxieties. It is no more helpful to position ourselves as 'better than'. If we think we are better than our clients we can end up patronising them and unable to see their strengths. The more we accept and esteem ourselves with all our imperfections the easier it is to accept our clients 'just as they are'.

BOUNDARIES

I believe it is essential for us as counsellors to have good boundaries. By good I mean both firm and flexible. A simple example of this is time-keeping. If a counsellor keeps to the time she has set aside for the counselling session a client feels safe. Emotions can sometimes be overwhelming and it helps the client to know that there is a limit to the time he has to spend on their expression and exploration. If the counsellor continually runs over time he may feel that she has no control and therefore that anything could happen. However, as I said, I believe a good boundary is also flexible. If the counsellor occasionally extends the session, it can be appropriate, provided: (1) she does it in full awareness, as a choice; (2) she explains what she is doing and why to the client; (3) she does not then overstep the extension.

It may be that the client is in extreme distress, or that he is feeling suicidal, or that the counsellor wants to include something like a visualisation and decides the session should be sixty, not fifty minutes. I should stress that she should consider the above check-points first and that it should be the exception and not the rule. If it is happening more frequently, supervision is needed to help you work out why your boundary has broken down, and how to get it back.

Boundaries are not just about time-keeping. If our own emotional boundaries are not good we may respond inappropriately to a client. For example, when a client is recounting an episode of physical abuse, if your own emotional boundary is too thin you might experience your client's pain to the extent that you feel a need to comfort them and remove their pain in order to make your own pain more bearable. This would prevent the client being allowed to experience his own feelings. On the other hand if your own emotional boundary is very inflexible you might shut down on hearing your client's expression of pain and be unable to empathise or even listen properly.

If we have a poor physical boundary we may be unable to respond helpfully. For example, if a client is testing out their sexuality with us by being sexually provocative: if your own sexual boundary is too thin you might feel you do not have a right to identify or challenge behaviour in your client which you do not think is appropriate. Or you might find that you not only feel aroused by your client's sexual approaches but respond to them directly or indirectly. In either case both you and your client are likely to feel unsafe if you do not: (1) name what you think is happening; and (2) gently but firmly point out that whilst it is ok to explore what this means in your relationship it cannot be acted upon. Equally, if your sexual boundary is too inflexible you might communicate to your client, however indirectly, that sex and sexuality are taboo subjects not to be explored with you. Whilst your client may well take his cue from you in order to gain your approval, and not repeat his sexually problematic behaviour in front of you, a communication, and the chance to explore its immediate and wider meaning, will have been missed.

If you are a co-dependent counsellor who is still using an addiction to hide from your real self, be it drink, drugs, relationships, food or anything else, you may be capable of living a manageable life and of being a reasonable counsellor. However, some parts of your life will certainly be unmanageable, and you will be out of touch with many of your feelings. When you are ready to give up your addiction you will be taking the first step towards resolving your co-dependency. You will also be taking the first step towards becoming a better counsellor.

Finally as you work on your own co-dependency you will begin to recognise and identify your co-dependent clients. You will ask more questions about addictions. You will begin to understand that your client is as hooked on his addict partner as she is on her drugs. You will think twice when your client describes his childhood as happy and uneventful. You will know how to teach your client about boundaries when he complains about his friends criticising him. You will have a new theory and practice which will enable you to make sense of, and work with what before seemed like a crazy and destructive way of life for many of your clients.

DISCUSSION ISSUES

1 What brought *you* into counselling?
2 Which issue in the above chapter is most pertinent to you?
3 How can you improve your boundaries as a counsellor?
4 Does this book throw new light on any of your clients, past or present? What might you do differently?

References and Further Reading

Assagioli, Robert (1965), *Psychosynthesis*, New York: Psychosynthesis Research Association, Hobbes, Dorman & Co. (Visualisation)

Beattie, Melody (1987), *Co-dependent No More*, Hazelden Foundation. (Co-dependency)

Bradshaw, John (1988), *Healing the Shame that Binds You*, Deerfield Beach, FL: Health Communications. (Shame)

—— (1991), *Homecoming*, London: Piatkus. (Inner child)

Cutland, Liz (1985), *Kick Heroin*, London: Sky Books and Bath: Gateway Books. (Co-dependency)

Dryden, W. and Golden, W. (eds) (1986), *Cognitive-behavioural Approaches to Psychotherapy*, London: Harper & Row. (Rational-emotive therapy)

Erikson, Erik H. (1964), *Childhood and Society*, New York: W.W. Norton & Co. (Child development)

Jeffers, Susan (1987), *Feel the Fear and Do it Anyway*, London: Random Century Ltd. (Self-image)

Kareem, Jafar and Littlewood, Roland (1992), *Intercultural Therapy*, Oxford: Blackwell Scientific Publications. (Racism)

Kasl, Charlotte Davis (1990), *Women, Sex and Addiction*, London: Mandarin. (Co-dependency)

Mellody, Pia (1989), *Facing Co-dependence*, San Francisco: Harper & Row. (Co-dependency)

Miller, Alice (1987), *The Drama of Being a Child*, London: Virago. (Loss of self)

Subby, Robert and Friel, John (1990), *Co-dependency and Family Rules*, Deerfield Beach, FL: Health Communications. (Co-dependency)

References and further reading

CHAPTER 2

Pia Mellody first acknowledged the confusion between co-dependency and love addiction. She has just brought out a book on this: *Facing Love Addiction* (HarperCollins, 1992), which clarifies the differences and addresses the recovery process from this particular addiction.

John Bradshaw writes more fully about 'shame-bound control' in Chapter 3, 'The hiding places of toxic shame' of his 1988 book, *Healing the Shame that Binds You*.

The idea of relapsing 'in awareness' is taken from 'The steps to recovery' in Charlotte Kasl's 1990 book, *Women, Sex and Addiction*.

CHAPTER 3

The idea of detaching in love or in anger is taken from Chapter 5, 'Detachment' of Melody Beattie's 1987 book, *Co-dependent No More*.

CHAPTER 4

The idea of education and writing work to identify childhood abuse is well known in treatment centres based on the 12-step principle. Pia Mellody writes fully about this systematic method in Parts 3 and 4 of her 1989 book, *Facing Co-dependence*.

CHAPTER 5

Susan Jeffers wrote about the use of a 'book of abundance' in Chapter 10, 'Choosing love and trust' of her 1987 book, *Feel the Fear and Do it Anyway*.

Index

Index